GOD AND YOU

God And You

KNOWING GOD AND OURSELVES

Daryl C Cyrus Jr

Dedicated to my wife and kids

GOD AND YOU

The Two Most Important Questions For You To Know

DARYL C. CYRUS, JR

Table of Contents

God And You

By: Daryl C Cyrus Jr

Preface

I have found my journey of faith to be one with plenty of ups and downs and twists and turns and yet I always inevitably come back to a point when I ask myself who is God, and who am I in relation to him. As you go through this book if you are someone just beginning to dive into faith, I hope this book can help you gently break the surface of the water. If you are a seasoned swimmer when it comes to faith, I hope this book reminds you of the truths you already know and in reminding you of what you already know maybe perhaps you'll discover something new as well.

Part 1 Who Is God?

1

Chapter 1: God The Trinity

There is no question more important for you to figure out than "Who is God?" Also, once you figure out the answer to that question, the second greatest question you can ask yourself is "Who are you in relation to God?" If you can answer these two questions correctly, I am positive you will live a life that you can be proud of, a life that will impact others in a godly way, and give you confidence when you stand before Christ one day and have to give an account on the life that you have lived.

A.W. Tozer once wrote, "What comes into our minds when we think about God is the most important thing about us."[1] I would like to argue that one of the things that should come first to our minds as Christians is the truth that we serve a triune God; in other words, the Trinity should be one of the first things to enter our minds when we think of God. Timothy George rightly argues in his article *The Nature Of God: Being, Attributes, And Acts* that when one talks about theology, the topic of the Trinity should come up early; otherwise, people will think that the Trinity is something of a lesser matter and will not devote time to thinking on it.[2] With all this talk on the Trinity, you might first think, what is the Trinity after all? In this section, I will give a brief history of the Trinity, provide scriptural support for the Trinity, and discuss how the truth of the Trinity affects our daily lives.

When Christians discuss the Trinity, we are saying, as John Chrysostom stated that the Father is God, the Son is God, the Spirit is God, and that God is one.[3] As Henry C. Thiessen puts it, "The Athanasian Creed expresses the trinitarian belief thus, 'We worship one God in the Trinity, and the Trinity in unity; we distinguish among the persons, but we do not divide the substance.' It goes on to say, 'The entire three persons are coeternal and coequal with one another, so that....we worship complete unity in Trinity and Trinity in unity."[4] Or, to make this simpler, the Trinity that Christians worship is one God who has revealed himself in three distinct, separate but equal persons: God the Father, God the Son, and God the Holy Spirit. When we say God is a "person," a helpful distinctive needs addressing from Driscoll and Breshears, "To clarify, to say that each member of the Trinity is a 'person' does not mean that God the Father or God the Spirit became human beings. Rather, it means that each member of the Trinity thinks, acts, feels, speaks, and relates because they are persons and not impersonal forces. Further, each member of the Trinity is equally God, which means they share all the divine attributes, such as eternality, omniscience, omnipotence, and omnipresence."[5]

With so much discussion on the Trinity, you might be surprised to hear that the Bible never uses the word Trinity. The concept of the Trinity is within the pages of the Bible, as we shall later see, but for the word Trinity to sum up this concept, we give thanks to a man named Tertullian. Tertullian was a popular theologian who lived from AD 155-220. What made Tertullian such a famous theologian? Tony Lane gives insights into this by writing, "Tertullian was the first important Christian to write in Latin. He is the father of Latin, Western theology......he was one of the greatest Latin writers ever, and it is said that pagans used to read his works simply to enjoy the style.......Or as a modern author said, Tertullian possessed an ability rare among theologians: he is incapable of being dull'!".[6] Tertullian spent much of his time writing against the Monarchians. The Monarchians denied the reality of the Trinity and stressed the 'monarchy' or sole rule of God; the Monarchians, they were strict monotheists.[7] For the Monarchians, the Trinity does not exist as three persons representing one God, but one God with three titles. To understand this belief, picture a man who functions as a husband, father, and son. To battle this incorrect view of God, Tertullian "…initiated the use of the Latin words, *Trinitas, persona, and substantia* (Trinity, person, and substance or essence) to express the biblical teaching that the Father, Son, and Holy Spirit are one in divine essence but distinguished in relationship as persons with the inner life of God himself.".[8]

As I wrote earlier, the Trinity is a concept we see within the pages of the Bible, and the first reference to the Trinity is in the first book of the Bible, Genesis. In Genesis 1:26 it says, "**[26]Then God said, 'Let us make human beings[a] in our image, to be like us. They will reign over the fish in the sea, the birds in the sky, the livestock, all the wild animals on the earth,[b] and the small animals that scurry along the ground.**"[9] Before God created humanity, he paused, and notice, he used the word "us." The "us" that God is referring to is to God The Son and God the Holy Spirit. You might be wondering how we can be confident of this truth. The answer is to remember God created you and me and the rest of humanity in his image. Later on, we will discuss what it means to be an image bearer of God, but for now, keep in mind that angels are not made in the image of God, and that the only thing that is made in the image of God is humanity.

Another place in the Bible where we see another reference to the Trinity is in the final book of the Bible, Revelation. In Revelation 1:4, John writes this greeting, "**…..Grace and peace to you from him who is, and who was, and is to come, and from the seven spirits of God, and from Jesus Christ, who is the faithful witness, the firstborn from the dead, and the ruler of the kings**

of the earth."[10] Alan F. Johnson, in his commentary on Revelation, rightly points out that the greeting that John is writing in Revelation is an expanded form of the Christian trinitarian greeting with "From him who is, and who was, and is to come" being a reference to God the Father, and "From the seven spirits of God" being a reference to the Holy Spirit.[11] When reading the Bible, remember that Genesis is about our creation in many ways and that Revelation is about the completion of our salvation. With that said, we see that each member of the Trinity worked together in bringing about our creation and that each member of the Trinity is at work in bringing about our eternal salvation. Driscoll and Breshears summarize this thought quite well by asserting, "As we grow to more deeply understand the saving plan of God the Father, the sacrifice of Jesus Christ, and the sealing of the Holy Spirit, we become more intimately thankful to each member of the Trinity for their work for us, in us, and through us."[12]

In his work Introducing Christian Doctrine, 2nd Edition, Millard J Erickson boldly states, "The doctrine of the Trinity is crucial for Christianity. It is concerned with who God is, what he is like, how he works, and how he is to be approached."[13] The Trinity is important, as Erickson states, because it helps us understand who God is. I would also like to add that by better understanding the Trinity humbly, we will better understand ourselves, since we are image-bearers of God. When it comes to how the Trinity affects our lives, I can think of no greater practical area than in the area of community. Driscoll and Breshears state, "The Trinity is the first community and the ideal for all communities."[14]

Before there was a creation, before there was time, love existed because our triune God has always existed; and because he has always existed, there has never been a time, nor will there ever be a time, when community has not existed. First John 4:7 says, **"⁷Dear friends, let us love one another, for love comes from God,** "and later on in First John 4:16, John simply tells us that God is love. John can tell us that God is love because God has always and will always live within perfect relationship within himself through the Trinity. It is recorded during the baptism of Jesus in Matthew 3:16-17: "[16]**As soon as Jesus was baptized, he went up out of the water. At that moment heaven was opened, and he saw the Spirit of God descending like a dove and alighting on him.** [17]**And a voice from heaven said, 'This is my Son, whom I love; with him I am well pleased.'**"[15] In the baptism of Jesus, we see all three members of the Trinity present, enjoying one another, and in complete unity with one another. When it comes to our relationships, they are all touched by sin, and none of our relationships are as healthy as they should be. For our relationships to thrive in our communities, we must look to the ideal relationship and the community that is found within God to help us in our relationships. At this time, I think it is appropriate to mention that we can see now that God did not create us because he was lonely. God created us to invite us into the relationship that has always existed, marked by love, unity, and community, with the hope that by living well with God, we will live well with one another.

As we bring this opening chapter to a close, I want to say that if any of this discussion of the Trinity is confusing to you, well, you are in good company. I believe the Trinity does not receive the attention it deserves because it is a rather complex concept for us as humans to wrap our minds around. Erickson once wrote, "Among the religions of the world, the Christian faith is unique in making the claim that God is one and yet there are three who are God."[16] Regarding the Trinity and other matters in the Bible, we should leave some room for mystery in our theology. Deuteronomy 29:29 says, "[29]**The secret things belong to the LORD our God, but the things revealed belong to us and to our children forever, that we may follow all the words of this law.**"[17] In some ways, the Trinity is not meant to be fully understood; it is meant to be a part of the secret things of God. However, enough of the Trinity is revealed to us so that we can worship our triune God as he has revealed himself to us throughout the Bible. I believe one more quote from Erickson on this topic is beneficial for us to close this chapter on the Trinity. "As someone has said of this doctrine: Try to explain it, and you'll lose your mind; But try to deny it, and you'll lose your soul."[18]

2

Chapter 2: God The Father

The first person of the Trinity is God the Father. Right now, I can only assume that perhaps someone reading this book would have an issue with God being referred to as a father. In *Heart Of A Father*, Wayne Holmes presents why so many are troubled with viewing God as a father by writing, "For many people the image of God as Father isn't a pleasant one because the image of their earthly father wasn't pleasant. Some view fathers as distant, uninvolved, and uncaring persons. Others remember an evil man who molested them, physically and/or emotionally. Still others picture a strict disciplinarian who relentlessly pushed them, never offering words of encouragement or love."[19]

The other problem people might have with viewing God as Father is how they interpret the Bible, mainly the Old Testament. It seems that in our world today, the vast majority of sermons, bible studies, and devotionals are focused on the New Testament; even one highly influential pastor once campaigned that Christians should "unhitch" their faith from the Old Testament. The reason is that the Old Testament is more foreign to us than the New Testament due to the period and culture it was written in. Michael A. Grisanti, in his chapter of The

World And The Word entitled "The World Of The Old Testament," points out that the Old Testament covers a period of 1,000 years from 1400 BC to 400 BC and that the culture of the Old Testament was the culture of the Ancient Near East.[20] In *Is God A Moral Monster?*, Paul Copan quotes well-known atheist Richard Dawkins who has this view of God in the Old Testament, "The God of the Old Testament is arguably the most unpleasant character in all fiction: jealous and proud of it; a petty, unjust, unforgiving control-freak; a vindictive, blood-thirsty ethnic cleanser; a misogynistic, homophobic, racist, infanticidal, pestilential, megalomaniacal, sadomasochistic, capriciously malevolent bully."[21] I would assume that anyone reading this book would disagree with Dawkins about God being a fictional being; however, outside of that, there might be some temptation within us to have questions about the goodness of God within the pages of the Old Testament, and maybe that is one reason it is often neglected by Christians today.

When our earthly fathers and, at times, our faulty view of the Old Testament might have failed us, how do we get an accurate view of God the Father? I believe the best way to get a precise view of God the Father is first to see what He says about himself. In Exodus 34:6, a conversation between God and Moses is recorded: **"The LORD passed by before him and proclaimed: 'The LORD, the LORD, the compassionate and gracious God, slow to anger, and abounding in loyal love and faithfulness."**[22] God says everything that one could want within a father when speaking about himself. The exciting thing about Exodus 34:6 is that when the character of God is brought up, this exact or similar wording is found in Numbers 14:18, Second Chronicles 30:9, Nehemiah 9:17, and Jonah 4:2.[23] God, throughout the Old Testament, wants people to know that He is good. In the following few pages, we will look at a couple of Old Testament examples to see God's goodness.

If you have ever spent time in church or Christian circles, then you are familiar with the story of Jonah. The danger of becoming too familiar with a story in the Bible is that our hearts can become dull to the events of the story because we can fall into the temptation of believing we have heard everything that a familiar Bible story has for us. It is my hope and prayer that as we look at the events in the life of Jonah, God uses the things that we are familiar with in Jonah and, at the same time, gives us the ability to look at Jonah with a fresh set of eyes so that we can see God for who he truly is.

With all this said, if we were to have a conversation and I asked you what Jonah was truly about, I wonder what answer you would have. Some people would say that Jonah is about running from the call of God; some other people would answer that Jonah is about facing our fears; others would say Jonah is about racism, or perhaps you would say it's about second chances, or you just might go with the tried-and-true answer that Jonah is about God causing a fish to swallow a man. For the record, I know that people debate whether it was a fish or a whale that swallowed Jonah; however, I have always enjoyed the answer that it was some aquatic beast that swallowed Jonah, but for the sake of this book, let's just use the word fish. All the answers so far have a measure of truth to them. Well, except for the aquatic beast. That's just no good, but I do think, when we look at Jonah, we can find a better answer to what it is about.

In Jonah 1:1 it says, "**¹The word of the LORD came to Jonah son of Amittai: ²Go to the great city of Nineveh and preach against it, because its wickedness has come up before me.**"²⁴ This verse is self-explanatory and simple to understand in many ways. God called Jonah to preach against Nineveh because Nineveh was wicked. How wicked was Nineveh, you might be wondering. Nineveh was the capital of the nation of Assyria, and in his chapter on Jonah, Mark F Rooker shares a quote from King Asshur-banipal on what he once did to those who opposed him, "I tore out the tongues of those whose slanderous mouths had uttered blasphemies against my god Ashur and had plotted against me, his god-fearing prince....The others, I smashed alive with the very same statues of protective deities with which they had smashed my own grandfather Sennacherib — now (finally) as a (belated) burial sacrifice for his soul. I fed their corpses, cut into small pieces, to dogs, pigs, *zi bu* birds, vultures, the birds of the sky and (also) to the fish of the ocean."[25] Faced with such brutality, Jonah ran from the mission that God had called him to Tarshish. It is believed that Tarshish was most likely located in modern day Spain and that it was in the exact opposite direction of Nineveh, with Nineveh being east and Tarshish being west. In fact, during the days of Jonah, Tarshish was known as the edge of the world.[26] As I wrote earlier, Jonah was running from the mission that God called him to, but there is more to it than that. Jonah was not only running from the mission that God had for him, but he was also trying to run from the God who gave him the mission.

In Jonah's attempt to flee from God and the mission that God called him to, he did not make it very far. Through God's control over nature, God cause a storm so violent that in order to stop the storm, Jonah was tossed out of his boat by his fellow shipmates. While Jonah was in the ocean and in fear of drowning, God, once again in display of his power over creation, sent a fish to swallow Jonah. There is no other way to describe it, but Jonah, through his own disobedience to God, found himself at rock bottom....I wonder if you could ever relate to Jonah in that, due to your own choices, have you ever found yourself in over your head? Even though Jonah was literally in the belly of a fish, I can only imagine metaphorically, have you ever found yourself in the belly of a fish?

For those of us who have found ourselves in the belly of a fish, pay attention to what Jonah does. In Jonah 2:1, it says, "**¹From inside the fish Jonah prayed to the LORD his God.**" When Jonah found himself in a horrible situation, he prayed. There are many things that Jonah did wrong, and we should not follow in his footsteps. However, the one lesson we can take from Jonah himself is to pray when we are in over our heads.

T. W. Hunt wrote on prayer, "Prayer must be built on the foundation of the sovereignty and character of God."[27] Jonah could have hope in prayer because he had hope in the character of God. What is the character of God? Psalm 103:8-13, which King David wrote and a psalm that Jonah would have had access to, describes God as, **"⁸The LORD is compassionate and gracious, slow to anger, abounding in love. ⁹He will not always accuse, nor will he harbor his anger forever; ¹⁰he does not treat us as our sins deserve or repay us according to our iniquities. ¹¹For as high as the heavens are above the earth, so great is his love for those who fear him; ¹²as far as the east is from the west, so far has he removed our transgressions from us. ¹³As a father has compassion on his children, so the LORD has compassion on those who fear him."**[28] Psalm 103:8 quotes Exodus 34:6 while describing God and then builds on that by comparing God to a compassionate father. Once again, some of us might never associate our fathers with the word compassionate; however, God wants us to know Him as a compassionate father whom we can run to and not run from when rock bottom situations happen. All of this leads to one of my favorite verses in all of scripture: Jonah 3:1, **"Then the word of the LORD came to Jonah a second time:"**[29] Jonah found himself out of the belly of the fish, and God came to Jonah a second time with the same mission of heading to Nineveh. God had every right to be done with Jonah, but he lavished grace upon Jonah. As Psalm 103 mentioned, God does not deal with us as our sins deserve, because every act of disobedience we do is deserving of judgment, but instead, God offers grace and comes to us a second time.

What does Jonah do with this second opportunity from God? Well, he carries out God's mission for him by telling Nineveh, **"Forty more days and Nineveh will be overthrown."**[30] Jonah's sermon is eight words in English and five words in Hebrew[31] , yet this message deeply impacted the King of Nineveh who personally repented and called for his entire nation to beg God for compassion and mercy. When God sees the actions of the Ninevites, it is recorded in Jonah 3:10, **"¹⁰When God saw what they did and how they turned from their evil ways, he relented and did not bring on them the destruction**

he had threatened.[32] God had promised that Nineveh would be destroyed but did not carry out that threat; how does that all work? One way to understand this is by examining the well-known story *The Christmas Carol.* When it comes to *The Christmas Carol,* there are many different adaptations, but still, the all-time best version is the Muppet version, and I have no shame in saying that. If you don't believe me, put this book down and watch it now. I'll be here when you get back…..or maybe just watch it once you're done reading this chapter. Anyways, Scrooge is visited by three ghosts on Christmas Eve, and each shows him his Christmases from the past, present, and future. With the visit of the Ghost of Christmas Yet To Come, Scrooge is shown his death and the death of a loved one, and while seeing these visions, Scrooge asks, "Are these the shadows of the things that will be, or are they shadows of things that may be only?" Because Scrooge changed his ways he was able to avoid a grim future. Because Nineveh changed its ways, it was also able to avoid a grim future as well.

What is Jonah's reaction to the success of his mission? Instead of being filled with joy at the salvation of Nineveh, Jonah 4:1-3 unfortunately contains these words, **"¹But to Jonah this seemed very wrong, and he became angry. ²He prayed to the LORD, 'Isn't this what I said, LORD, when I was still at home? That is what I tried to forestall by fleeing to Tarshish. I knew that you are a gracious and compassionate God, slow to anger and abounding in love, a God who relents from sending calamity. ³Now, LORD, take away my life, for it is better for me to die than to live."**[33] Jonah is angry with God because he is the exact opposite of what Dawkins or any atheist believes; dare say that at this moment, Jonah was longing for God to be what Dawkins believes God to be. Instead, Jonah was greeted by the God of the Bible, who wants to save lives and not destroy them. In fact, at the very end of the book of Jonah, God is trying to get Jonah to see things from his perspective in Jonah 4:11, the final verse in Jonah's story. God has this to say, **"¹¹And should I**

not have concern for the great city of Nineveh, in which there are more than a hundred and twenty thousand people who cannot tell their right hand from their left ----- and also many animals?"[34] God tells Jonah there are over 120,000 people who do not know the difference between their right and left hands. Who are these 120,000 people? Well, some commentators will say that it refers to people who are spiritually blind, while others make the case that the 120,000 refer to small children; whatever the case, God is telling Jonah there are people in Nineveh he wants to show mercy to, and not just them but the animals as well.

I asked earlier what the story of Jonah truly is about. One pastor once told me years ago that the story of Jonah is not about God causing a fish to swallow a man, but it's about God causing a man to swallow his pride. Because God is a compassionate and gracious father, God is trying to save not only Nineveh but also Jonah from the destructive pride in him that made him think he knew better than God. The God of the Old Testament is not a moral monster; he is very far from that. However, he is the gracious and compassionate father who chases after his wayward children and seeks to be merciful to those in rebellion against Him.

Going back to Exodus 34:6, I really enjoy the NET translation of this verse. I particularly like this translation because it talks about the type of love that God has. The NET translation of Exodus 34:6 says God possesses loyal love. God does not love us with a love that is capricious or a love that fades away. God loves us with a love that is loyal. One of the best stories in the Bible that shows loyal love comes from the life of the prophet Hosea. Unlike Jonah, the story of Hosea might be something you are unfamiliar with; however, Hosea is a showcase of the heart of God.

Hosea 1:2-3 states, **"²When the LORD began to speak through Hosea, the LORD said to him, 'Go, marry a promiscuous woman and have children with her, for like an adulterous wife this land is guilty of unfaithfulness to the LORD.' ³So he married**

Gomer daughter of Diblaim, and she conceived and bore him a son."[35] This is shocking to read, and I don't just mean that God called Hosea to marry an unfaithful woman, but that someone would actually name their daughter Gomer. I have never met a woman with the name Gomer my entire life, and I'm going to assume that you haven't either. In the unfortunate and scarce scenario that a woman named Gomer is reading this book, I apologize for making fun of you, and I am sure your parents never read Hosea when it came to naming you Gomer.

Seriously though, the opening verses of Hosea are pretty shocking in that God would call one of his prophets to marry an unfaithful woman. Even though the NIV uses the word promiscuous to describe Gomer, other translations carry far stronger words, such as the ESV, which refers to Gomer as "a wife of whoredom" and the NASB1995 as "a wife of harlotry," and the NLT goes as far as calling Gomer a prostitute. Due to the overall shock and bizarreness of this odd pairing of Hosea and Gomer, some commentators over the years, like the reformer John Calvin and the church father Jerome, believed the marriage of Hosea and Gomer was an allegory and not to be read as literal.[36]

What was the point of God commanding Hosea to marry Gomer? Through Hosea's relationship, God gave Israel a visual representation of the relationship God had with them, with Hosea representing God in his loyal love and Gomer representing Israel in her unloving and unfaithful ways. In what ways was Israel unfaithful to God? Hosea 4:1-2 reveals, **"Hear the word of the LORD, you Israelites, because the LORD has a charge to bring against you who live in the land: 'There is no faithfulness, no love, no acknowledgment of God in the land. There is only cursing, lying, and murder, stealing, and adultery; they break all bounds, and bloodshed follows bloodshed."**[37] The cycle of life within Israel broke the heart of God, just like Gomer would go on to break the heart of Hosea.

In what ways did Gomer break the heart of Hosea? Well, for starters, Gomer lived up to her reputation and took many romantic partners while being married to Hosea, to the extreme that Hosea couldn't be positive that he was the biological father of the children that lived in his home. Speaking of home, Gomer eventually abandons Hosea and leaves their home to pursue her many lovers. Unfortunately for Gomer, when she leaves Hosea, things in her life take a tragic turn, and she winds up being placed in an auction for enslaved people. Remember that Hosea represents God, and when Gomer left Hosea, life did not get better but worse for her. When Israel pulls away from God, the nation does not get better, it gets worse. When we wander away from God, we are worse off for it.

With such shame and humiliation, Hosea has every right to end his marriage with Gomer biblically. However, God comes to Hosea and relays this message to him in Hosea 3:1, **"Then the LORD said to me, 'Go and love your wife again, even though she commits adultery with another lover. This will illustrate that the LORD still loves Israel, even though the people have turned to other gods and love to worship them."**[38] God tells Hosea to love his wife again. Let your mind and heart soak that up for a moment. God wants Hosea to love an unfaithful wife because God loves a people who have been unfaithful to him. In this moment, God is having Hosea be a visual representation of what loyal love looks like.

I can only imagine what thoughts were going through the mind of Gomer while she was on the stage being bid for by men who had no good intentions for her. To add to her fear of being faced with life as a slave, she was also robbed of whatever dignity she had because the practice of that day was to strip women of their clothes so those who were bidding could make sure they were getting all of their money's worth.[39] I wonder if Gomer kept replaying in her mind the choices she had made that put her in this situation. I can almost guarantee the thought of Hosea coming to her rescue was inconceivable to her. I know Gomer represents Israel, but in many ways, Gomer is also a representative of us. I do not know about you, but when I screw up, God's loyal love does not come to my mind.

Switching gears for a moment, there was a time in the book of Isaiah when God brought judgment on his people, and, in response to that judgment Isaiah 49:14 tells us what they thought, **"Yet Jerusalem says, 'The LORD has deserted us; the LORD has forgotten us.'"**[40] In response to this, God reassures His people in Isaiah 49:15-16, **"¹⁵Never! Can a mother forget her nursing child? Can she feel no love for the child she has borne? But even if that were possible, I would not forget you! ¹⁶See, I have written your name on the palms of my hands. Always in my mind is a picture of Jerusalem's walls in ruins."**[41] When Israel thought God had forgotten them, God reminded them that he had a love for them that would not allow him to forget about them. God goes as far as to say he has their names written on the palm of his hands as a reminder. When we believe that God has forgotten us due to our poor choices, we must remind ourselves that we are written upon his heart.

Returning to Hosea and Gomer, how did Hosea demonstrate his loyal love for Gomer? In Hosea 3:2 it says, **"²So I bought her for fifteen shekels of silver and about a homer and lethek of barley."**[42] Hosea demonstrated his loyal love by redeeming Gomer from a lifetime of slavery. According to Exodus 21:32 and Leviticus 27:4, the going price for a female slave was thirty shekels of silver. Unfortunately for Hosea, it appears from the text that he was too poor and didn't have access to thirty shekels of silver and had to make up the difference with the equivalent of another fifteen shekels of silver with dried goods. According to *Time in the Word Ministries,* Hosea had to spend half a year's earnings to save Gomer. For Hosea to demonstrate loyal love to Gomer, it cost him dearly.

Hosea is a word picture for what God's loyal love looks like. Through Hosea the prophet we get to see God as a wounded spouse, but the book of Hosea also portrays God as a wounded father as well. In Hosea 11:1-4 God speaks for himself and listen to how he compares his relationship with Israel: **"¹When Israel was a child, I loved him, and** out of Egypt I called my son. **²But the more they were called, the more they went away from me. They sacrificed to the Baals and they burned incense to images. ³It was I who taught Ephriam to walk, taking them by the arms; but they did not realize it was I who healed them. ⁴I led them with cords of human kindness, with ties of love. To them I was like one who lifts a little child to the cheek, and I bent down to feed them."**[43] Can you hear God's pain as you read his words as he mourns over the condition of his relationship with Israel? He repeatedly says I loved my son. I taught my son how to walk. I looked over him and healed him. I lifted them up to my cheek so that I could kiss him. And yet in spite of God being an amazing father to Israel they want nothing to do with him. For any parent who has a fractured relationship with their children God fully understands that pain. And for parents who have wayward children and who continue to love and sacrifice for them, God does that as well for his own rebellious children.

So far, we have seen the compassionate heart of God as a father from Jonah and Hosea. When it comes to seeing God as a father, maybe there is no one best suited to help us see God this way other than Jesus. Perhaps you have heard the parable of the Prodigal Son. However, I want to take some time to explain why Jesus told this parable, and maybe by understanding the background of this parable, we can appreciate this lesson from Jesus much more deeply. The reason why Jesus even told this parable can be found in Luke 15:1-2 which says, **"¹Now the tax collectors and sinners were all gathering around to hear Jesus. ²But the Pharisees and the teachers of the law muttered, 'This man welcomes sinners and eats with them.'"**[44] From verses 1 and 2, we see that Jesus is addressing two groups of people, with one group being the "tax collectors and sinners" and the other group being the "Pharisees and the teachers of the law." Observing this should make us pause and question how we have traditionally heard about this parable of Jesus. Perhaps by understanding the two groups of people, we can better understand what Jesus is trying to accomplish in his teaching.

When it comes to tax collectors, can we just agree that nobody grows up as a kid wanting to be a tax collector? Being a tax collector is something people just stumble into unfortunately, and it is a universally hated profession. I have never in my life met anyone eager to encounter a tax collector. Well, in the days of Jesus, tax collectors were hated as well, but the reason why tax collectors were despised was multi-layered. One reason they were so despised is that it was common practice for tax collectors to charge more than the government required, and they would keep the extra money for themselves. However, what really caused tax collectors to be hated by their fellow Jews was that they worked for the Roman government, which was actively oppressing the Jewish people. Due to this, many Jews viewed tax collectors as traitors to their people and mercenaries for Rome who picked money over loyalty to their own people.[45] When it comes to sinners, I know we all view each other as sinners, so that word doesn't carry much weight for us today. However, in the first century, to be labeled as a sinner meant you belonged to a designated group of people. This group of people cared nothing about even attempting to follow God and would actively live in opposition to the rules of God.[46]

The second group of people that Jesus was dealing with were the Pharisees and the teachers of the law. The word Pharisee means "separated ones," and they were militant in keeping God's laws as the teachers of the law interpreted them.[47] The Pharisees trace their origin back to a group known as the Hasidim, which arose in the second century B.C. During this point in history, the Syrian King Antiochus IV tried to abolish the Jewish religion. The Hasidim joined with other Jews, led by Judah Maccabee and successfully revolted against King Antiochus IV. This restoration of Jewish worship is celebrated by Jews today during the holiday of Hanukkah.[48] During the days of Jesus, the Pharisees were the largest and most influential Jewish group.

With that background information out of the way, let's return to the parable Jesus taught. Before Jesus gets to the Prodigal Son, he tells the story of a lost sheep that a shepherd searches for, and a story of a lost coin that a woman searches for. When both the shepherd and woman find the lost sheep and the lost coin, there is great rejoicing because the lost things have great value. This sets the stage for the story of the Prodigal Son. The Father of the story has two sons, and the younger son asks his father for his part of the inheritance before his father dies so that he can spend it. Picking up the story from there, Luke 15:13-16 says, **"[13]Not long after that, the younger son got together all he had, set off for a distant country and there squandered his wealth in wild living. [14]After he had spent everything, there was a severe famine in that whole country, and he began to be in need. [15]So he went and hired himself out to a citizen of that country, who sent him to his fields to feed pigs. [16]He longed to fill his stomach with the pods that the pigs were eating, but no one gave him anything."**[49] So far in this parable, we have seen the younger son take the wealth his father gave him and completely waste it, living contrary to his father's wishes. At this point in the story, we know that the younger son is truly lost. Remember the other two parables Jesus taught with the lost sheep and lost coin. When the sheep was lost, someone searched for it. When the coin was lost someone went to search for it. The younger son is lost, and between a lost sheep, a lost coin, and a lost person, it is the person who has the most value. Also, remember that the father has another son, the elder son, who should be searching for his younger brother. Unfortunately, though we are told in verse 17 **"When he came to his senses, he said, 'How many of my father's hired servants have food to spare, and here I am starving to death! [18]I will set out and go back to my father and say to him: Father, I have sinned against heaven and against you. [19]I am no longer worthy to be called your son; make me like one of your hired servants.' [20]So he got up and went to his father."**[50] Jesus tells us that the younger son had to come to his own senses and realized the plight of his situation. Once again, out of a lost sheep, a lost coin, and a lost person, it is the person who has the most value; yet, the one who possessed the most value, was the one nobody looked for. The reason why the older brother was not searching for his younger brother was that he was also lost as well. In reality, the story of the Prodigal Son should be called the Prodigal Sons. This is a story of how a father relates to his lost sons, two sons who are lost in different ways.

How does the father relate to the lostness of his younger son? Jesus tells us that when the father saw his son a distance off, that he was filled with compassion at the sight of his son, ran to him, and embraced and kissed his lost son. This would have been shocking behavior for the original hearers of this story. The reason why this would have been shocking was that, in that culture, a father would have waited for his son to address him first and show him some form of respect.[51] What Jesus reveals about God is that God's love is willing to defy social norms and is extravagant! Jesus is also teaching that for those who have wandered away from God and chosen an openly rebellious lifestyle, the heart of God is that of a father who simply wants his children to make the journey home.

Remember that within this parable, there is not one but two lost sons. We've seen how the father relates to the younger son, but what about the lostness of the older son? When it comes to the older son, when he heard of how his father rejoiced over his brother's return and threw a celebration in his honor, Jesus shares the older brother's reaction in Luke 15:28-30, **"[28]The older brother became angry and refused to go in. So his father went out and pleaded with him. [29]But he answered his father, 'Look! All these years I've been slaving for you and never disobeyed your orders. Yet you never gave me even a young goat so I could celebrate with my friends. [30]But when this son of yours who has squandered your property with prostitutes comes home, you kill the fattened calf for him!'"**[52] Jesus shows us that when the older son refused to come to the party of his younger brother, the father was willing to leave the party and plead with his firstborn to attend the party. What I find revealing is the answer to why the older son is so angry with his father. The older son reveals that for years he slaved and worked for his father, and according to him, his father never gave him anything. It is here we see why the older son is also lost as well. Even though the older son never left home and openly rebelled as his younger sibling did inwardly, he was far from his father; he was far from home. Even though he had an outward loyalty to his father, he had never truly given his heart to his father. What this parable reveals is that lostness can come in various ways. Some have an open rebellion as the younger brother possessed, while others are like the older brother who outwardly play the part of a dutiful son quite well but inwardly are desperately far away, lost in the acts of service without a relationship.

The ending of this parable ends in one of the worst ways possible, with a cliffhanger. Jesus tells us the father pleads with his older son by saying, **"'My son,' the father said, 'you are always with me, and everything I have is yours. But we had to celebrate and be glad, because this brother of yours was dead and is alive again; he was lost and is found.'"**[53] We have no idea how the older son responded to his father's pleadings. Honestly, I believe the reason for this is that for us, it is not important how the older brother responds, but it is important how we respond. Through the examples of Jonah, Hosea, and through the parable of Jesus, we see the heart of God as a compassionate and merciful father. When it comes to God, will you view him as Dawkins does as the malevolent bully of the universe, or will you embrace God as the Bible reveals him as the one who desires to be your eternal father?

3

Chapter 3: God The Son

When it comes to Jesus, what can I possibly write to do him justice? The Apostle John, at the end of his gospel, wrote, **"Jesus did many other things as well. If every one of them were written down, I suppose that even the whole world would not have room for the books that would be written."**[54] With that said, there is no way I can cover every nuance about Jesus in this chapter. However, I hope to cover his life in such a way that we have a better understanding of who he is and what he should mean to us. While reading this chapter, if you find yourself longing to know more about Jesus, that is an incredibly good thing, and I pray that this chapter can be a launchpad for you to pursue Jesus with a greater desire. With that said, what should come to our minds when it comes to Jesus? I think one of the first things that should come to our minds are the words of John the Apostle, who wrote in John 1:1-3, **"¹In the beginning was the Word, and the Word was with God, and the Word was God. ²He was with God in the beginning. ³Through him all things were made; without him nothing was made that has been made."**[55] In the opening verses of his gospel, John refers to Jesus as "the Word", so in reality, we could read John 1:1-3 this way as well: "In the beginning was Jesus, and Jesus was with God, and Jesus was God. Through

Jesus, all things were made; without Jesus, nothing was made that has been made." John stresses in his opening that Jesus is fully God and, as the Second Person within the Trinity, had a part in the creation of everything that is in existence. The Apostle Paul in Colossians 1:16-17 bolsters this claim by writing, **"[16]for all things in heaven and on earth were created by him – all things, whether visible or invisible, whether thrones or dominions, whether principalities or powers – all things were created through him and for him. [17]He himself is before all things and all things are held together in him."**[56] When we think of Jesus, we should always have near the forefront of our mind that Jesus is fully God and that everything in creation owes its existence to Jesus. Not only does everything owe its existence to Jesus, but everything, including me and you were created by him and not only by him, but more importantly for him. As Saint Augustine of Hippo once wrote, "You have made us for yourself, and our heart is restless until it rests in you."[57]

The second truth we must keep in mind about Jesus is that he is fully one of us, a human being. One of the greatest truths of the Bible is that of the incarnation of Jesus, of God becoming a human being. Humanity is made in the image of God, and Jesus, being the creator, decided to bear the image of his creation by becoming a human. On Jesus becoming a human, author Philip Yancey, in his book The *Jesus I Never Knew*, wrote, "The God who came to earth came not in a raging whirlwind nor in a devouring fire. Unimaginably, the Maker of all things shrank down, down, down, so small as to become an ovum, a single fertilized egg barely visible to the naked eye, an egg that would divide and redivide until a fetus took shape, enlarging cell by cell inside a nervous teenager."[58] I cannot help but get caught up in the idea that Jesus left the glory and luxury of heaven to make his home for nine months inside the womb of his mother, Mary.

When Jesus would emerge from Mary's womb, what type of reception would he receive from the world that he created? Unfortunately, John pens these words for us when it comes to how Jesus was received by the world, **"He was in the world, and the world was created by him, but the world did not recognize him."**[59] When Jesus was born, there was celebration amongst the angels, but amongst the realm of men outside of Mary, his step-father Joseph, and some shepherds, business carried on as usual. Jesus, the King of Kings, worthy of all the thrones of the earth at his birth, spent his first night on the planet as a human in an animal's feeding trough.

When you think of Jesus going through life as a human, what images come to your mind? I know growing up, I saw all sorts of pictures of Jesus, and in each picture, Jesus would stick out from everyone else, and in some pictures, he would even have a glow about him or even a halo. In fact, my grandma has a picture of Jesus with long flowing hair, and he is a rather attractive guy, and his picture is right between former president Barak Obama and Martin Luther King Jr……you know, just the way your grandma has her picture of Jesus set up!

The Bible gives us quite a different portrayal of Jesus than modern pictures do. The Bible shows Jesus in his humanity as quite ordinary, in the sense that if Jesus were in a crowd, he probably would not stick out to you. John the Baptist, when thinking about Jesus, would say, **"I didn't know he was the one, but when God sent me to baptize with water, he told me, 'The one on whom you see the Spirit descend and rest is the one who will baptize with the Holy Spirit.' I saw this happen to Jesus, so I testify that he is the Chosen One of God."**[60] What John the Baptist is telling us is that Jesus was so human that, apart from God the Father making it painfully obvious, he would not have suspected Jesus to be God's son. In all honesty, this shouldn't be as surprising to us because 700 years before Jesus would become a man, the Prophet Isaiah wrote, **"There was nothing beautiful or majestic about his appearance, nothing to attract us to him."**[61] There are fake gospels that exist that talk about the childhood of Jesus, such as the *Infancy Gospel of Thomas,* which makes claims that Jesus would do outlandish things such as make birds from clay, blind people that annoyed him, and kill kids that ticked him off (don't worry he would later resurrect the kids he killed). For many reasons, the *Infancy Gospel of Thomas* was rejected from the Bible; one, it was not written by the Apostle Thomas, and another was for the cartoonish and out-landish image of Jesus it sought to create. In many ways, though, this fake gospel reveals the temptation of the human heart to discredit the genuine humanity of Jesus. As we seek to worship Jesus as God, we, too, must be careful not to deprive him of his humanity.

What was life like for Jesus as a human? Once again, John the Apostle gives us a not-so-great image of what life was like for Jesus by writing, **"He came to what was his own, but his own people did not receive him."**[62] Jesus came into a world that did not recognize him, and he came to a people that were created by him and for him, and he was greeted with rejection. I think it is fair to mention at this point that Jesus was not only faced with death in his adult years but there were people longing to seek the death of Jesus while he was still an infant. One of the people who sought the life of Jesus while he was still a child was Herod the Great. To be perfectly honest, there are not too many great things to say about Herod. If you are not familiar with Herod, he was a paranoid king who ruled in Judea and was desperate to keep his crown at all costs. Due to his paranoia, he ended up putting to death two of his brothers-in-law, his own wife Mariamne, and two of his sons.[63] Herod was so cruel to his own family that Emperor Augustus once said, "It's better to be Herod's pig than his son." Herod's cruelty extended far beyond his own family. When he was close to death, he ordered the arrest of numerous citizens, and when he died, these people were also to be put to death as well. Herod did this because he wanted to guarantee there would be an appropriate amount of mourning on the day of his death.

Why did Herod the Great desire the death of baby Jesus? Matthew, in his gospel, recounts how Herod became aware of Jesus due to the Magi who came to visit him, seeking Jesus who had been born in a hope to worship him. Herod saw Jesus as a threat to his throne, but, in the presence of the Magi, he feigned interest in wanting to worship

Jesus with the hope that the Magi, once they discovered where Jesus was, would relay that information back to him, and then he would have his opportunity to kill Jesus. Knowing Herod's intention for his son, God warned the Magi through a dream not to share any knowledge of Jesus with Herod and they went back to their home a different way. Once Herod found out that he had been duped, he went into a rage and, with the information that he had, sought the death of every male age two and under in Bethlehem and the surrounding area. Mary, Joseph, and Jesus were able to avoid this bloodshed because an angel appeared to Joseph in a dream and told him of Herod's plot to kill Jesus and instructed Joseph to carry his family to Egypt. Even though Herod failed to claim the life of Jesus, he did manage to claim the lives of many other children during his heinous actions in Bethlehem. This was such a horrific action Matthew would quote from the Prophet Jeremiah and write, **"A voice was heard in Ramah, weeping and loud wailing, Rachel weeping for her children, and she did not want to be comforted, because they were gone."**[64] Jesus, from the moment breath entered his lungs, had people who wanted his death. The God who created everything visited his creation as a man and received a less than cordial welcome with unrecognition and rejection.

One of the greatest and most difficult mysteries in all scripture is how Jesus is fully God and fully man. How on earth did these two natures exist in one person? On pondering this great mystery, Erickson wrote, "This is one of the most difficult of all theological problems, ranking with the Trinity and the paradox of human free will and divine sovereignty."[65] We see in the temptation of Jesus, the tension of these two natures all at once. Jesus, being God, is perfect and cannot sin, but as a human, Jesus felt the pain of temptation, as do all who bear the mark of humanity. During our time together, we will not be able to resolve what others could not resolve in how Jesus' two contrasting natures find peace. However, I hope that we can appreciate the tension and mystery of it all and see how Jesus relates to us in our temptation and yet, as God, was fully victorious over temptation.

Something we must remember when reading the temptations that Jesus faced is what happened before Satan tempted him. Before the events of his temptation, the baptism of Jesus took place. When we look upon the baptism of Jesus, we should, in a sense, see it as a coronation in his life because God the Father publicly states that Jesus is his beloved son. After God's glowing endorsement of Jesus, Matthew wrote, **"Then Jesus was led by the Spirit into the wilderness to be tempted by the devil."**[66] The previous chapter in the Gospel of Matthew ended with the Father throwing elaborate praise on Jesus; why on earth, in the very next chapter of Matthew, would the Holy Spirit lead Jesus into the wilderness to be tempted by Satan? In fact, Jesus, in the model prayer, says we should pray **"And lead us not into temptation."**[67] The very prayer Jesus says we should pray, the very opposite of that prayer happened to him. The Holy Spirit led Jesus into the desert, according to the Father's will, to be tempted by Satan. One way to make sense of all this is to keep in mind what happened after the temptation of Jesus. After Jesus was victorious over Satan, he began his public teaching and healing ministry. As one pastor once told me, before God uses a person greatly there is normally a time of great testing. Chances are, before you will ever do great things for God, you too will also find a great season of testing in your life. Before God would use his own son greatly, he allowed Jesus to face great testing as well.

As Christians, we believe Jesus has been tempted just as we have been tempted. However, at first glance, the temptations of Jesus seem to have little in common with the temptations we face in life. Jesus was tempted to turn stones into bread, to throw himself from a building so that an angel could save him, and to worship Satan to inherit the kingdoms of the world. To properly understand the nature of Jesus' temptation and how these temptations relate to us, we must go back to the dual nature within Jesus. In Philippians 2:6-7 Paul describes Jesus as, **"[6]Though he was God, he did not think of equality with God as something to cling to. [7]Instead, he gave up his divine privileges; he took the humble position of a slave and was born as**

a human being..."[68] Jesus, being fully God in his decision to become a man, decided to put himself completely under the authority of God the Father as a slave. In other words, Jesus would not do anything that his Father did not permit. Even the miracles that Jesus would perform during his earthly ministry were under the Father's authority. This is why when Jesus talks about his second coming in Matthew 24:36, which says, **"However, no one knows the day or hour when these things will happen, not even the angels in heaven or the Son himself. Only the Father knows."**[69] This does not pose a problem because as God, Jesus knows all things, but, in his humanity, he had given up the divine privilege of his abilities and only had access to them as the Father desired.

With everything we have discussed, look back at the temptations that Jesus faced. By turning stones into bread, Satan wanted Jesus to use his authority over the natural world. By casting himself off a high place and commanding an angel to rescue him, Satan wanted Jesus to assert his power over the spiritual world. Within the final temptation of worshiping Satan and Satan telling Jesus he would give him the kingdoms of the world, he was trying to get Jesus to receive worship on his own, apart from the Father. In these temptations, Satan wants Jesus to cast off the authority of his Father and to be God on his own terms. The temptation to be independent of God and to do life on our own terms is the same temptation he gave to Adam and Eve in the Garden of Eden, it is the same temptation he gave to Israel in the wilderness, and this is the same temptation he gives to me and you every time we are tempted. In this way, Jesus relates to us and has been tempted just as we are tempted. Charels Spurgeon once wrote, "God only had one sinless Son, but not one child who did not suffer the rod of trials. What great comfort and confidence come from knowing that Jesus has been tempted in every way, just as we are."[70] When temptation comes your way, and trust me it will, take hold of the advice given to us in Hebrews 4:14-16, **"[14]Therefore, since we have a great high priest who has ascended into heaven, Jesus the Son of God, let us hold** firmly to the faith we profess. [15]For we do not have a high priest who is unable to empathize with our weaknesses, but we have one who has been tempted in every way, just as we are — yet he did not sin. [16]Let us then approach God's throne of grace with confidence, so that we may receive mercy and find grace to help us in our time of need.[71]

Let's make one thing clear Jesus had more than twelve followers in his life, although he had twelve followers to be with him full time. Why did he have twelve followers to be with him full-time? Mark 3:14-15 says, "[14]And he appointed twelve (whom he also named apostles) so that they might be with him and he might send them out to preach [15]and have authority to cast out demons."[72] One reason why Jesus had twelve followers with him was so that he could have human company. People are not meant to live alone. People are meant to have community with one another. According to one study, 62.3% of the world's population uses social media, with a daily average of 2 hours and 23 minutes.[73] In fact, on the night that he was betrayed, Jesus took Peter, James, and John, who were the disciples that he was closest to, and confided to them, "My soul is deeply grieved, even to the point of death. Remain here and stay awake with me."[74] With Jesus being a part of humanity, we should not find it strange that, like all of us, he, too, desired a genuine connection with other humans. The second reason Jesus had twelve full-time disciples was that he could equip them for ministry. These followers of Jesus would be entrusted to carry on the work of his ministry when he returned to heaven. These men were so successful in carrying on the work of Jesus, in spreading the gospel, that 2,000 years later, here we are discussing Jesus as you read this book.

What are some things that we learn about these men in relation to Jesus and the calling he had for their lives? An interesting observation can be made from reading Matthew 17:24-27. Within the passage's context, there is a conversation about paying a temple tax. According to Jewish law, every male between the ages of twenty and fifty had to pay the temple tax.[75] From the passage the thing that stands out is that only Jesus and Peter had to pay the tax, which means the rest of the disciples either had payment for the tax or were exempt from the tax. From Luke 3:23, we know Jesus was about thirty when he began his public ministry, and the custom of his day was that a religious teacher would have students who would be younger than him. This makes the possibility that the vast majority of the twelve apostles were under the age of twenty, apart from Peter.

With everything we have discussed so far, let's briefly look at how Jesus shaped one of his twelve apostles, John. When it came to John and his brother James, Jesus gave them the nickname Sons of Thunder.[76] As cool as that name would be for a wrestling brother tag team, that is not why Jesus gave that nickname, and James and John were not the first renditions of Thor and Loki. From this nickname, we can assume that John struggled with anger like many young men. In Luke chapter 9, it's recorded that Jesus and his disciples once went to a Samaritan village. At this village, they received less than a warm welcome, to the point that both John and his brother James went up to Jesus and said, **"Lord, do you want us to call fire down from heaven and consume them?"**[77] In all translations, the response that Jesus has is that he corrects the brothers, but I love the response that Jesus has in the King James translation, which is, **"For the Son of man is not come to destroy men's lives, but to save them."**[78] What a response from Jesus! John, as a young man who struggled with anger, but at the same time wanted strongly the approval of Jesus, received the original come to Jesus talk. Jesus might have bruised John's ego that day, but he also gave him a life lesson that he never forgot. For when John was an elderly man, he wrote 1John and in 1 John 4:7-8, **"⁷Dear friends, let us continue to love one another, for love comes from God. Anyone who loves is a child of God and knows God. ⁸But anyone who does not love does not know God, for God is love.**[79] John, who was a brash and angry young man at one point in his life, transformed into a man known for grace and love. This metamorphosis took place because John spent meaningful time with Jesus. As we follow Jesus, he too will change us as he changed John. Whether your struggle is anger, lust, jealousy, or whatever it is, Jesus desires to work in our lives to help us to become the people we were always meant to be, like he helped John to become the person he was always meant to be.

At this point, I have a confession I want to make to you. I have been steeped in Christian culture since I was a kid, and I currently work in ministry. I want to tell you that a part of me is completely over it. I am not over God. If I were, I wouldn't be writing this book, but when it comes to the evangelical Christian subculture I am a part of, I find myself in a state of delusion. The reason for this is that I have found life to be an incredibly messy process, and I do believe that Christianity in Western culture tries its best to present one side of life and tries to disassociate itself from the messiness of life. I'm old enough to remember the tragedy of 9/11 and the rippling effects of the aftermath. I remember after 9/11, churches were full of people, and then gradually, the rush of people into churches became a trickle, and then eventually, even the trickling stopped, and life went back to normal. I know many people bemoaned that the people who initially came to church stopped coming, but what if one reason they stopped attending wasn't out of malice for God, but because the messages they heard did not correspond to life as they knew it?

When I think about the life of Jesus, I think of the sobering words of Isaiah 53:3, "**³He was despised and rejected— a man of sorrows, acquainted with deepest grief. We turned our backs on him and looked the other way. He was despised, and we did not care.**"[80] Nobody knows how messy life can be better than Jesus. Nobody knows how ugly life can be better than Jesus. There is nobody better equipped to help navigate through the messy and ugly side of life outside of Jesus. When Isaiah prophesied that Jesus would, in a sense, have a messy life and that he would be a man of sorrows and grief, did that surprise you? When I first encountered the words of Isaiah and read Jesus's life in the gospels, it was a shock. After the shock of reading the life of Jesus faded away, I felt a sense of relief. The Jesus I had been taught for a good portion of my adolescent life was an individual who had a pristine life; the Godman who had everything given to him was a myth. In reality, Jesus struggled mightily. If you are someone who has experienced the ugly side of life, take comfort in Jesus, and let's explore some examples from his life.

Jesus grew up under a stigma that followed him his entire life. What was the stigma that followed Jesus wherever he went? In John chapter 8, Jesus is having a heated conversation with a group of people. At one point in this conversation, the crowd responded to Jesus with, **"We were not born of sexual immorality."**[81] Also later on in the same chapter in verse 48 they say to Jesus that he was a Samaritan. The stigma that Jesus had to deal with for his entire life were the details behind his birth. Due to the supernatural birth of Jesus, the rumor mill of his day was that Mary was unfaithful to Jospeh prior to their marriage and that Jesus was a product of Mary's unfaithfulness. By saying that Jesus was a Samaritan the crowd was calling into question the ethnicity of Jesus and once again questioning the legitimacy of this birth.[82] One outspoken critic of Christianity during the second century was the Greek Philosopher Celsus, who speculated that Jesus was a byproduct of Mary having an affair with a Roman soldier named Panthera.[83] Like many people today who question the virgin birth of Jesus, there were people in the days of Jesus who also questioned his birth and, when the opportunity would arise, would mock him to his face about the details of his birth.

Another messy challenge that Jesus found himself having to navigate through were issues with his family. For some people, including myself, family can be a trying thing to work through, and Jesus was no exception. It should be noted that from reading Matthew 13:55 and Mark 6:3, Jesus did not grow up as an only child but had half-siblings, James, Joseph, Simon, and Judas, and some sisters who were unnamed. The issue that caused tension within the family of Jesus were his claims of being the Messiah. In Mark 3:20-21, it's written, **"²⁰One time Jesus** entered a house, and the crowds began to gather again. Soon he and his disciples couldn't even find time to eat. **21When his family heard what was happening, they tried to take him away. 'He's out of his mind,' they said."**[84] Outside of Mary and Joseph, none of Jesus's immediate family believed what he stated about himself until after his resurrection. Prior to his resurrection, as you can tell from the text you've just read, the brothers and sisters of Jesus believed that he was insane for claiming that he was the son of God. In John 7:1-5, Jesus's brothers mock him right in his face about claiming to be the Messiah, and all their hostility is found in verse 5, which says, **"For even his own brothers did not believe in him."**[85] One time, while preaching, Jesus once said, **"Do not think that I have come to bring peace to the earth. I have not come to bring peace but a sword. For I have come to set a man against his father, a daughter against her mother, and a daughter-in-law against her mother-in-law, and a man's enemies will be the members of his own household."**[86] What Jesus meant by the words that he spoke is that he realized that the message he preached possessed the power to bring people together but it also had the potential to cause division amongst people, even family members. I wonder when Jesus spoke those words, was he picturing the conflict that his message caused within his own family? The hostility was so great between Jesus and his siblings that, from what we can tell from scripture, not one of them was present at the crucifixion of Jesus to support Mary, and Jesus told the only disciple present at the crucifixion, who was John, to look out for his mother. There are truly no wounds like family wounds, and Jesus knew this unpleasant truth intimately.

With all this discussion of family hostilities, there was one family member whom Jesus seemed to get along with, and that was his cousin John the Baptist. As we have discussed earlier in this chapter, John was the one who baptized Jesus and was one of the first people to recognize Jesus for who he truly wass. By all accounts, John was a just man, but unfortunately for John, he found himself living in an unjust world. Being a just man, John found himself confronting one of Herod the Great's sons, Herod Antipas who became a ruler once he died. John confronted King Herod because he had taken his brother's wife to be his own. Being an unjust king, Herod did not appreciate what John had to say to him and threw him in jail. Once Jesus was made aware that John was behind bars, he heaped praise onto John by saying, **"I tell you the truth, of all who have ever lived, none is greater than John the Baptist."**[87] While John received the highest praise that one can get, it still did not stop Herod from taking his life by having him beheaded. We are told by the Apostle Matthew, who was an eyewitness to this event, that once Jesus heard the news of his cousin's death, he got into a boat to head towards a remote area so that he could be alone.

I remember one time having a meal with a family after I conducted the funeral services for one of their loved ones. During this meal, I was sitting with a woman I did not know, and she told me that her sister had been murdered by her ex a couple of years ago and that her niece was the one who discovered her. My heart broke for this woman, for the funeral she was experiencing that day, and for the continual funeral that took place in her heart for her sister. All I can think right now is there are many in this world, just like this woman who have lost loved ones who were full of life in unjust ways, and maybe you are someone who has experienced this pain as well. Jesus knows what it feels like to have a loved one murdered and the messiness of having to deal with such a tragedy.

With all the mess of life that Jesus experienced, nothing was messier than the cross. In the time period of Jesus, there was no worse way to die than suffering death upon a cross. The Romans did not create the horrors of crucifixion, but they did perfect it. Cicero, who was a Roman statesman, scholar, and writer before the time of Jesus's incarnation, had this to say about the cross, "It is a crime to put a Roman citizen in chains, it is an enormity to flog one, sheer murder to slay one: what, then, shall I say of crucifixion? It is impossible to find the word for such an abomination.[88] Cicero found the cross to be so barbaric at another time he wrote, "…. And the very word 'cross,' let them all be far removed from not only the bodies of Roman citizens but from even their thoughts, their eyes, and their ears."[89] The cross that brought such indignation from Cicero was the death that Jesus endured.

Why did Jesus have to endure the cruelty of the cross? The short answer is because there was no other option. The night before Jesus was crucified, he prayed to God the Father that if there was any option besides the cross, he wanted that path, but, because there was not, he entrusted himself to his heavenly father's plan. In the book of Hebrews, we are told this about Jesus and the cross, **"Because of the joy awaiting him, he endured the cross, disregarding its shame."**[90] What was the joy that awaited Jesus? The joy that awaited Jesus on the other side of the cross was that by his death, he would guarantee our salvation and, by doing so, would bring glory to God the Father. What I find truly amazing about Jesus and the cross is that throughout his ordeal on the cross, Jesus has concern for others and not himself. While being crucified, Jesus prays for those who are killing him, comforts another man who is being crucified with him, and even makes sure that his mother is taken care of prior to his death. By all accounts, Jesus lived an incredibly difficult life, but not once do we ever see him give way to bitterness or self-resentment. Nobody had it harder than Jesus but also nobody had more joy than Jesus. Jesus lived his life in such a way that kids wanted to be around him, women felt safe in his presence, and men aspired to be better versions of themselves because of him. It is not surprising that Jesus died as he lived in his final moments, being a light to all mankind.

Jesus, who was the light of the world, had his light snuffed out by the very world he came to save. If the story of Jesus ends with the cross, then it is a tragedy like no other. However, the story does not end with his death; it culminates in his victory through the resurrection, which is the single most important event in human history. Christianity rises and falls on whether the resurrection happened or not. The Apostle

Paul wrote, **"And if Christ has not been raised, your faith is futile."**[91] Christianity does not rise or fall with one's view on creation. Christianity does not rise or fall on one's view of the end times. Christianity rises and falls on whether Jesus was raised from the dead or not. Well-known 20th-century atheist Bertrand Russell, who rejected Christianity, once wrote, "That Man is the product of causes which had no prevision of the end they were achieving; that his origin, his growth, his hopes and fears, his loves and beliefs, are but the outcome of accidental collocations of atoms; that no fire, no heroism, no intensity of thought and feeling, can preserve an individual life beyond the grave; that all the labors of the ages, all the devotion, all the inspiration, all the noonday brightness of human genius, are destined to extinction in the vast death of the solar system, and the whole of Man's achievement must inevitably be buried beneath the debris of a universe in ruins---- all these things, if not quite beyond dispute, are yet to nearly certain, that no philosophy which rejects them can hope to stand. Only within the scaffolding of these truths, only on the firm foundation of the unyielding despair, can the soul's habitation henceforth be safely built."[92] Bertrand Russell embraced a worldview in which life happened by accident, and nothing that one actually achieves in life matters because everything is rushing to the unyielding despair of death. The Christian worldview gives hope to those who place their hope in Jesus. The hope is that because he died and rose from the dead, then death is also not our final chapter, as it was not the final chapter for Jesus. *The Lord Of The Rings* author, J.R.R. Tolkien, once famously said, "The birth, death, and resurrection of Jesus means that one day everything sad will come untrue."[93] What a promise to hold on to. Because Jesus lived, died, and rose again, all the sad events in our lives do not have to define us, but one day, they will be untrue because of Jesus.

4

Chapter 4: God The Holy Spirit

I have another confession to make to you. The confession I would like to make to you is that I like Star Wars. At one point in my life, I thought I loved Star Wars, but that was until I met people who actually loved Star Wars, and I realized my relationship with Star Wars is not one based off love, but simply like. What I enjoy about Star Wars is the idea of good versus evil, a wide universe to explore, multiple characters with multiple stories, and the idea of wizards in space who fight with laser swords. As much as I am a fan of Star Wars, I fear it might have affected how some of us view God, mainly the third member of the Trinity, the Holy Spirit. For many, the Holy Spirit is the most mysterious member of the Trinity and the least understood. Some have even gone as far as seeing the Holy Spirit as a force, akin to Star Wars, as a power to be wielded by Christians.

When we look at the Holy Spirit, we must keep the words of J. Dwight Pentecost in mind, "However, no subsequent study in the great doctrines of the work of the Holy Spirit will mean much to you personally unless you realize that we are considering One who is as much a Person as God the Father or God the Son. The Holy Spirit is as much a Person as you are or I am."[94] As previously mentioned, what I mean by person is that the Holy Spirit has an intellect, will, desires, a thought process, and emotions. In this regard, the Holy Spirit is a person as we are persons as well, and he is not an arbitrary force that one can wield at their leisure. It is my hope as we investigate the person and work of the Holy Spirit that maybe we can remove some, but not all, of the mystery of the Holy Spirit because He is still God, and there will always be some mystery when it comes to God. I do hope that we can better understand, appreciate, and fall more in love with this mysterious person of the Trinity.

Forty days after Jesus rose from the dead, he ascended back to heaven. I can only imagine the emotions of the disciples as they watched Jesus rise into the sky and enter the glories of heaven. I wonder if the disciples had a sense of joy for Jesus and, at the same time, a sense of uneasiness about what it meant for them. I wonder if they felt a sense of grief at watching the one they loved, the one they had recently gotten back from death, only to lose him once again to heaven. Augustine, on the ascension, had this to say, "You ascended from before our eyes, and we turned back grieving, only to find you in our hearts."[95] How can Jesus reign from heaven and simultaneously reign in our hearts as well? This is possible through the work of the Holy Spirit. On the night of his betrayal, Jesus had an interesting talk with the disciples and said to them in John 14:16-17, **"And I will ask the Father, and he will give you another advocate to help you and be with you forever— the Spirit of truth.**[96] During that same night, Jesus would tell the disciples in John 16:5-7, **"⁵But now I am going to him who sent me, and none of you asks me, 'Where are you going?' ⁶But because I have said these things to you, sorrow has filled your heart. ⁷Nevertheless, I tell you the truth: it is to your advantage that I go away, for if I do not go away, the Helper will not come to you. But if I go, I will send him to you."**[97] How on earth was it an advantage for Jesus to leave the disciples? How on earth is it to our advantage that Jesus isn't physically present with us? I do not know about you, but I have a hard time accepting what Jesus is saying here. Nevertheless, Jesus does not lie, and Jesus is never wrong. If Jesus told the disciples that it was to their advantage that he would not be physically present with them, then it was to their advantage, and it is to our advantage as well.

How is it to our benefit not to have Jesus physically present with us? The answer is that we have the Holy Spirit. In the two passages of John that I referred to, the Holy Spirit is called both a helper and an advocate. In other translations, such as the APMC, he is called the counselor and the comforter. The Greek word that is being translated that encapsulates all the different references to the Holy Spirit is the word paraclete. In *The Mystery Of The Holy Spirit*, RC Sproul shares this insight on the word paraclete: "The term paraclete had a rich and varied usage in the ancient world. The word is derived from a prefix (*para-*) and root (*kalien*), which together mean 'one who is called alongside.'"[98] The Holy Spirit is the one who comes alongside us as an advocate, a counselor, a helper, and a comforter. In this way, Jesus did not abandon us on earth as he went back to heaven, but he left us the best representative in his place, and in this way, it is to our advantage that Jesus ascended to heaven so that the Holy Spirit could come alongside us.

In John 15:26, Jesus spoke on the Holy Spirit, saying, **"²⁶But I will send you the Advocate, the Spirit of truth. He will come to you from the Father and will testify about me."**[99] One of the Holy Spirit's main responsibilities is to point people to Jesus. In fact, if it was not for the Holy Spirit working in people's lives, no one would be a follower of Jesus, and that includes both you and me. In *The Deep Things Of God*, Fred Sanders recounts the story of one-time famous gang member turned evangelist Nicky Cruz who wrote, "God is a magnificent Father. God is a magnificent Saviour, Jesus Christ. But if it were not for the magnificent Holy Spirit, I would still be a wretched, hateful sinner! It is not enough to have a Father God who loves and provides for me. It is not enough, even to have a Saviour who died for my sins. For any those blessings to make a difference in our lives, there must also be present in this world that Third Person of God, the

Holy Spirit."[100] The Holy Spirit is the one who convicts us of sin and is the one who makes the message of salvation in Jesus attractive to us. Cruz goes on to say about the Holy Spirit and his work in salvation, "Jesus saved me; the Father forgave me. But the Holy Spirit convicted me, brought me to my knees, and showed me God....He showed me Jesus Christ, and I was gripped by His strong, sweet love. And then He shoved me toward God, and I gladly fell into the arms of my loving Father."[101] Throughout his earthly ministry, Jesus made references to the Holy Spirit and made much of Him. Now the Holy Spirit in his ministry makes much of Jesus in pointing humanity towards him.

With all this talk of the Holy Spirit in the New Testament, we need to remind ourselves that the Holy Spirit was also very active in the Old Testament. The work of the Holy Spirit was prominent when it came to the kings of Israel. As part of Saul's ascent as the first king of Israel, 1Samuel 10:10-11 says, "**[10]When he and his servant arrived at Gibeah, a procession of prophets met him; the Spirit of God came powerfully upon him, and he joined in their prophesying. [11]When all those who had formerly known him saw him prophesying with the prophets, they asked each other, 'What is this that has happened to the son of Kish? Is Saul also among the prophets?'"[102]** The Holy Spirit came upon Saul so that the people of Israel would all publicly recognize him as king, and through the influence of the Holy Spirit, Saul was able to lead Israel. Later on in Saul's reign, he began to turn away from God and made poor choices to the point that God rejected him from being king, and we are told these fateful words in First Samuel 16:14, "**[14]Now the Spirit of the LORD had departed from Saul....."[103]** With the influence and power of the Holy Spirit no longer working in Saul's life, everything that was once good within his kingship took a downward spiral, and Saul would never recover from this moment.

It then should be no surprise to us when David, who was the second king of Israel, found himself in a state of rebellion against God and prayed, "**Do not cast me from your presence or take your Holy**

Spirit from me."[104] There is a belief amongst some Christians that David is concerned about losing his salvation, and that is why he prays to God not to remove the Holy Spirit. However, keep in mind everything David knows at this point. David knows that when the Holy Spirit departed from Saul, he lost the kingdom. With that in mind, I would like to suggest that David is not praying about his salvation when he asks God not to remove the Holy Spirit from him. He is, however, praying that God does not remove the Holy Spirit from him because he knows that without the Holy Spirit's influence, he cannot be the king that Israel needs, and like Saul, without the Holy Spirit, he will lose his kingdom.

In the Old Testament, the Holy Spirit came upon kings, prophets, and certain individuals to help them accomplish the tasks that God required them to perform, but he did not permanently reside within them; it seems he only worked within a select group of individuals. The promise of the New Testament is that the Holy Spirit is not just for a special group of believers but that he comes to all those who have placed faith in Jesus. He does not temporarily reside in those who are saved but permanently lives within them. Ephesians 1:13-14 says, "**[13]And you also were included in Christ when you heard the message of truth, the gospel of your salvation. When you believed, you were marked in him with a seal, the promised Holy Spirit, [14]who is a deposit guaranteeing our inheritance until the redemption of those who are God's possession- to the praise of his glory.**"[105] Notice that the passage states that the Holy Spirit seals us and that he is also called a deposit. In his commentary, Gerald Peterman mentions that in the ancient world, a seal meant that something was owned and protected.[106] Also, pay attention to the idea that the Holy Spirit is the deposit or, in other words, the down payment for our salvation. What the Bible is stressing is that we do not have to ever live in fear of the Holy Spirit departing from us as believers, as the kings of the Old Testament had to worry. The Holy Spirit, who is God, lives within believers. John Calvin was right in his assessment of the Holy Spirit when he wrote, "He is the seed and root of heavenly life in us."[107]

As we have already gone over, the Holy Spirit seeks to make much of Jesus. The question is, how does the Holy Spirit accomplish this? Well, the answer is rather shocking: the Holy Spirit makes much of Jesus through people. The Holy Spirit makes much of Jesus through me and you. In 1Corinthians 12:4, it says, "**⁴Now there are different gifts, but the same Spirit.**"[108] Every Christian is given a spiritual gift from the Holy Spirit that is meant to be used in helping to spread the saving message of Jesus. The three main passages in the bible that discuss the spiritual gifts are Romans 12:6-8, 1 Corinthians 12:4-11, and 1 Corinthians 12:28. Now a Christian can have more than one gift from the Holy Spirit, but every believer has at least one of the following gifts: prophecy, serving, teaching, encouraging, giving, leadership, mercy, word of wisdom, word of knowledge, faith, healing, discerning of spirits, speaking in tongues, interpretation of tongues, and helps.

With all this talk of spiritual gifts and how every Christian possesses one, you might be left with some questions. In particular, you might be wondering, especially if you have read the book of Acts and read about the miraculous activities that took place in the early church, why don't we see such things today? When it comes to spiritual gifts, Christians find themselves mainly divided between two camps. One camp, known as the cessationists, believes that some of the more charismatic gifts of the Holy Spirit, such as speaking in tongues and miraculous healings, were for a certain point in the church's life and no longer take place today. The other camp, which are called continuationists, hold to the belief that all the gifts of the Holy Spirit are relevant for today.

Often, when it comes to miracles, there is an assumption that a miracle is taking place on every other page of the Bible. In reality, though, there were only three periods in biblical history where miracles were prominent: Moses and the Exodus, the ministries of Elijah and Elisha, and Jesus and his apostles.[109] In the Old Testament, for example, well-known prophets such as Isaiah, Habakkuk, Jeremiah, and Ezekiel had no miracles to accompany their messages throughout their ministries.[110] In the New Testament, it should be noted that after the period of Jesus and the apostles, much of church history is rather scarce on the veracity of miracles. The age after the apostles was called the age of the Church Fathers, with one of these fathers being a man named Origen who had this to say about miracles, "Miracles began with the preaching of Jesus, were multiplied after his ascension, and then decreased; but even now some traces of them remain."[111] Everything we have gone over so far should make us pause and rethink our stance on miracles. We now know that miracles were not the common phenomena that some would make us believe they were. The question we should be asking is, if miracles were not even a common thing within the Bible, what purpose do miracles serve and what role does the Holy Spirit play in all this?

Robert L. Saucy, who once served as the Professor of Systematic Theology at Talbot School of Theology, made an interesting observation. Saucy observed that miracles in the Bible are often referred to as signs. According to Saucy, a sign is the following: "A sign is that which points to something else. What is crucial in a sign is not the sign itself but its functional character, which is designed to give credibility to something else."[112] When it comes to miracles, they were always meant to be a sign to point to something else and not meant to be an end to themselves. The miracles in Moses and the Exodus pointed to God as a mighty savior and that Israel was his chosen nation. In the ministries of Elijah and Elisha, the miracles pointed to God being the divine ruler and not the kings of Israel. In Jesus and the Apostles, the miracles pointed to the fact that Jesus was the Messiah and that the church was his chosen vehicle to spread his message.

Have you ever learned how to ride a bike? For me, the process is one of many traumatic memories from my childhood. Let's say I was a rather slow learner when it came to mastering how to ride a bike. I spent plenty of Saturdays in an elementary school parking lot being berated by my dad each time I fell from my bike....it doesn't help that I was twelve trying to figure this out. Like I said, I am a slow learner.

What does riding a bike have to do with miracles and the Holy Spirit? Well, when one is learning to ride a bike, they have training wheels and, for the record I was greatly acquainted with training wheels. Once someone knows how to balance on a bike, and for the record, I did manage to accomplish this, they no longer need training wheels. When it comes to miracles in the Bible, they took place to authenticate a work of God, but once the work of God was established, it seemed the miracles were no longer needed on a large scale. In this sense, miracles, like training wheels, were used to establish a new work that God was doing, but once the work was completed, God moved away from primarily using miracles.

What does all this mean for today? We live in a day and age in which people long to see miracles. I have personally heard from missionaries who have said they witnessed supernatural events that they could only explain as works of the Holy Spirit. In trying to make sense of all this, I have already talked about the two camps that Christians fall into when it comes to miracles and the gifts of the Holy Spirit: the cessationist or the continuist. There is, however, one more camp that Christians fall into: the open but cautious camp. The open but cautious view seeks to be a middle-ground view between the two other views. As the name of the position states, this view is open to the possibility that the more miraculous gifts of the Holy Spirit could exist in our world today; however, this view cautions against viewing everything as a miracle. When it comes to the spiritual gifts of the Holy Spirit, I would suggest that we do not want to put him in a box that states He cannot perform certain supernatural activities today as the church in Thessalonica once did. Paul had to tell them not to "quench the Spirit," which means cutting him off from the work He desires to accomplish.[113] However, we should not be looking to the Holy Spirit as if He is a magician putting on a magic show to entertain people as the church in Corinth did. If the Holy Spirit allows miraculous signs to occur, they are just that, signs. Signs that are meant to point us to worship Jesus.

Moving on from any controversies that Christians might have about the spiritual gifts, let's focus on what all Christians can agree on regarding the Holy Spirit. All Christians believe that the Holy Spirit resides in them and that life in the Holy Spirit should promote some change. What does life in the Spirit look like? Galatians 5:22-23 describes a life saturated in the Holy Spirit as the following, "**²²But the Holy Spirit produces this kind of fruit in our lives: love, joy, peace, patience, kindness, goodness, faithfulness, ²³gentleness, and self-control. There is no law against these things!**"[114] Notice what Paul does not write; he does not write "fruits," but he wrote "fruit." There are not different fruits of the Spirit, but one fruit accompanies all the characteristics that Paul mentioned. Oftentimes, I make excuses for my poor attitude, whether it be bouts of anger or just a lack of general goodness in my disposition. I don't know; maybe you share the same struggle as me when I say I am not a patient person. We both need to realize that because the Holy Spirit lives in us, we have access to all the qualities that He desires for us to have. As one Christian told me years ago, because of the Holy Spirit living in us, Christians should be known as the most generous people on the planet.

With everything we have discussed about life in the Spirit, why does the Christian life feel so disconnected from what it should be? Jesus once mentioned that the Christian life is like living water and that salvation is like living water bursting inside us. Why, then, does the life of a believer often feel dry and barren, like traveling through a desert? As we have seen in 1 Thessalonians 5:19, Paul wrote, "**Do not quench the Spirit.**" We can quench the Holy Spirit from working in our lives through, at times, our unbelief. Another thing worth looking at is the idea of possession. I do not mean to freak anyone out, but possession is real and biblical. In the Bible, when a demonic spirit possesses someone, there is no question that the person is possessed and that the demon is in charge. When someone is a Christian, we believe that the Holy Spirit lives in them; however, we cannot always tell if someone is a Christian through their actions. With the demon, there is no free will; the demon runs the show. With the Christian, the Holy Spirit seems to respect our free will, and at times, this cuts him off from what he desires to do in our lives.

I remember one time reading through the book of Ephesians and I came across a verse that rocked my view on God. In Ephesians 4:30, I read, **"And do not grieve the Holy Spirit of God, with whom you were sealed for the day of redemption."**[115] Think about this with me. The Holy Spirit, who is God who had a part in creating all the universe, the Spirit that rose Jesus from the dead, lives in us and requests that we do not grieve him. Through our actions, we can cause the Holy Spirit sadness. Once again, a reminder that the Holy Spirit often allows us to make decisions that personally cause him sorrow because he respects our decision-making process, even when he disagrees with it. With our choices, is it possible that the dryness we are experiencing is not because the Holy Spirit lacks a desire to work in us but that he is heartbroken?

At this point, there might be a part of you that is mourning the state of your relationship with God and let me encourage you that is not necessarily a bad thing. In fact, conviction is a very good thing that the Holy Spirit does for believers. What you want to do is to make sure that you are feeling conviction from the Holy Spirit and simply not depression. What is the difference between the two? In 2Corinthians 7:10, Paul gives this distinction, **"Godly sorrow brings repentance that leads to salvation and leaves no regret, but worldly sorrow brings death."**[116] In his kindness, the Holy Spirit will break our hearts over our sinful decisions but will not leave us in that condition. He will help us to change and move past our destructive tendencies. Worldly sorrow will only point out our flaws, and it will leave us in a condition which we know is bad but will offer no help to change.

At this point, I want to say something you might not believe. You might not believe it because there are days, I don't even believe it. However, just because we might struggle to believe in something does not change the fact that it is still true. In Philippians, Paul, who was in jail at the time for preaching the gospel, wanted to encourage the church in Philippi that he helped to plant. Paul, who could no longer be in person with them, but still desired for them to grow spiritually, wrote, **"For it is God who works in you, both to will and to work for his good pleasure."**[117] God takes pleasure in helping his children grow spiritually into the adults they are meant to be. Just because it is hard to believe, does not make it any less true. I do not know how you are doing spiritually but take to heart that God does not regret saving you and that God is working in you, and he delights in doing it. God is able to work in us through the person of the Holy Spirit. Jesus truly was correct when he told the disciples and us it was to our advantage that he went back to heaven so that the Holy Spirit could come. As Erickson once wrote, "The Holy Spirit is the particular person of the Trinity through whom the entire Triune Godhead works in us."[118]

Part II WHO ARE YOU IN RELATION TO GOD?

Part II WHO ARE YOU IN RELATION TO GOD?

5

Chapter 5: You Are Image Bearer

If you cannot tell by now, I am a sucker for movies. When Marvel was all the rage, you can bet I rode that bandwagon until it broke down. One of my favorite movies from the Marvel Cinematic Universe has to be the very underappreciated masterpiece that is Iron Man 2. We will not talk about the abhorrent mess that was Iron Man 3 and how they tried to massacre my boy, Tony Stark. One of my favorite scenes from Iron Man 2 is when Tony finds some footage that has his deceased father, Howard, in it and that Howard had recorded a message for him. This discovery is important because Tony had a very dysfunctional relationship with his father and believed he was nothing but a disappointment to Howard. However, as a complete shock to Tony, his father, Howard, tells him that he is his greatest creation.

What Tony was to Howard, we are to God. You and I, along with the rest of humanity, are God's greatest creation. I am very deliberate when I say that we are a creation of God. As Charles C Ryrie has written, "The act of creating man was based on the deliberate counsel of God….. Man was no afterthought, but the result of deliberate forethought on the part of the Godhead."[119] You are not an afterthought, and you did not arrive on this planet by mistake. You are here because of God's deliberate planning. How far does God's deliberate plan go for humanity? In discussing Christianity with a group of people, Paul, in Acts 17:26-27 said, "**[26]From one man he made all the nations, that they should inhabit the whole earth; and he marked out their appointed times in history and the boundaries of their lands. [27]God did this so that they would seek him and perhaps reach out for him and find him, though he is not far from any one of us.**"[120] Nations are made up of people, and from these two verses, we learn that God determines where people not only live on the planet but also what time periods they live in as well. Paul tells us that God did all of this with the hope that people would reach out to him. God has determined where you live on the planet, and God has determined what time in history you live in with the hope that you would reach out to him. Our lives are not accidental, but they are part of the deliberate planning of God.

In what ways is humanity unique? Well, one way is that we are neither solely physical nor spiritual creatures, but we are soul and body creations. God could have created us purely as spiritual beings as he and the angels are, but he chose not to do that. God chose to give humanity a physical body. In some religions and with some Christians, there is a dangerous tendency to place the spiritual over the physical or, in some sense, to downplay the needs of the physical. I remember one time hearing about a pastor in his attempt to share the gospel with a homeless man who told him that if he needed a cot, he could go to a shelter; if he needed food, he could go to a soup kitchen because all he had for him was the gospel to preach. I hope the story I heard about this pastor isn't true and that it is just a gross exaggeration. Unfortunately, though, I have a haunting feeling that the story is true and that many of us who profess Jesus as lord might have the same thought process as the pastor I heard about.

In attacking the dangerous idea that the physical doesn't necessarily matter, Vaughn Roberts, in his book *God's Big Picture,* wrote, "Matter matters because God made it; it is 'good.' He is interested not just in our souls but also in our bodies and the world we live in."[121] God is interested not only in our spiritual condition but also in our physical condition, and this is no better illustrated than the life of Jesus. In Matthew 9:35-38, it is written, "**35 Jesus went through all the towns and villages, teaching in their synagogues, proclaiming the good news of the kingdom and healing every disease and sickness. 36When he saw the crowds, he had compassion on them, because they were harassed and helpless, like sheep without a shepherd. 37Then he said to his disciples, 'The harvest is plentiful but the workers are few. 38Ask the Lord of the harvest, therefore, to send out workers into his harvest field.'"** From the verses in Matthew, we see that Jesus preached to people and that in his preaching and teaching, he addressed the spiritual needs of people; however, he did not stop there. We are told in the latter half of verse 35 that Jesus also healed people, and by healing people, he also addressed their physical needs. My favorite verse from this passage that pulls on my heart is verse 36. I love this passage because we are told that when Jesus looked upon a crowd of people, he had compassion for them because, according to him, they were like sheep without a shepherd to guide them. Jesus had compassion for both the spiritual and physical issues that plague people. Jesus went as far as to tell his disciples they should pray to God the Father to raise up more disciples who would be like him and care for people with their physical and spiritual problems.

What does it look like to care about the physical needs of people? Chances are you are like me, and neither one of us possesses the miraculous abilities that Jesus had. To know what it looks like to care for the needs of others, let's look at James, the half-brother of Jesus. As I have previously mentioned, James was a hardened skeptic of Jesus until he encountered his older brother after the resurrection. After encountering the resurrected Jesus, James placed his faith in his brother and would go on to become the pastor at the church in Jerusalem. While pastoring, James would confront the issue of the nature of faith and works that were a problem in his church by writing, "**What good is it,**

my brothers and sisters, if someone claims to have faith but does not have works? Can this type of faith save him? If a brother or sister is poorly clothed and lacks daily food, and one of you says to them, 'Go in peace, keep warm and eat well,' but you do not give them what the body needs, what good is it? So also faith, if it does not have works, is dead being by itself. But someone will say, 'You have faith and I have works.' Show me your faith without works and I will show you my faith by my works."[122]

What James informed his congregation and what we can glean from his wisdom is that we do what we can for people. One of the core elements of Christianity is that we genuinely care for people and seek to make the world a better place because of our faith in Jesus.

At this time, I will emphasize once again that we are not saved by what we do but by placing our faith in Jesus. Some individuals claim we are saved by doing good works and will use a passage like James to uphold that belief. There are others who will say that the Bible contradicts itself by claiming Paul and James have a different view of the nature of works and faith. In order to succinctly address this matter, I will tell you something I once heard while attending a class on understanding the Bible. While attending the class, the professor said, "The Bible was not written to us, but it was written for us." What that professor means is that when the Bible authors were writing the Bible, they were writing to a particular audience at the time who were the first recipients of their work. The authors of scripture were thinking of their original audience in writing and addressing the needs of that audience. In that sense, the Bible was not written to us; however, God knew that the messages in his word would go beyond the original audience and would be read to help believers well beyond the time of the original audience of the Bible. With that said, when it comes to Paul and the book of Romans, when Paul makes the case that works do not save an individual, he is emphasizing this point because he is dealing with an audience that is obsessed with doing works to earn their salvation. When James is writing to his audience, he is dealing with a group who believe that because they have faith, they do not need to be concerned with the issues around them. James is getting to the point of how someone can have faith but not care for the welfare of others; how on earth could that type of faith save them? James is declaring that true faith should show itself by caring for people.

In other words, James is saying social justice should matter to Christians. I know social justice is a loaded term in our society and carries much baggage. However, if we strip away all the excess to the term social justice, it is simply caring for the physical needs we see in the world. Missionaries Willaim Carey and William Cameron Townsend understood this principle well. William Carey, in his efforts in India, addressed the spiritual needs of the people by sharing the gospel, and in turn, the physical benefits were that the practices of infanticide and burning widows with their deceased husbands came to an end.[123] Likewise, Townsend, in his efforts to share the gospel in Guatemala, would not only start a school but would also add a medical clinic, set up a generator for electricity, a plant to process coffee, and a supply store for agriculture.[124] Townsend would do all this because he believed it would help him in his efforts to share the gospel by showing the people he cared about their spiritual problems along with their physical problems. When it comes to Christianity, we need to remember that God cares not only about the spiritual but also the physical. If we ever need a reminder, we just need to remember that God has created you and me as body and soul creatures, and both matter to God.

As humans, we are fascinated by the spiritual realm. One area of the spiritual life that people seem not to be able to get enough of is angels. When it comes to Christmas cards at Christmas time, baby Jesus might be front and center, but you will find numerous cards with angels as well. I have been to enough funerals at this point in my life to know that someone who means well will probably say that their deceased loved one died because God needed another angel in heaven. Even when it comes to romance, a man might refer to the woman in his life as his angel. At this time, I would like to mention to any women who might be reading this that if a man says you look like an angel, you might want to smack him. This is because, in the Bible, an angel is either always portrayed as a male or as something that strikes fear into its observer. As a woman, being called an angel should never be taken as a compliment!

With all this fascination with angels, we should not be surprised that David, who wrote Psalm 8, pondering about humanity within its place in creation, wrote: **"When I consider your heavens, the work of your fingers, the moon and the stars, which you have set in place, what is mankind that you are mindful of them, human beings that you care for them? You have made them a little lower than the angels and crowned them with glory and honor."**[125]

How can humanity be God's greatest creation when David, in his psalm, wrote that God has created us a little lower than the angels? To answer this question, we need to see Psalm 8 within the light of the rest of the Bible. An obsession with angels is not something new to our time, but even in the days of the New Testament, people struggled with proper admiration of angels. In the book of Hebrews, the author makes this statement concerning angels and their relationship to Jesus, **"So he became as much superior to the angels as the name he has inherited is superior to theirs."**[126] The author of Hebrews has to make the case that Jesus is greater than the angels because people thought angels were superior to people, and if Jesus came in the form of a man, then he was less important than an angel.

Even though angels might have abilities greater than people, they are not in themselves superior to humanity. To make this point, Hebrews 1:14 says, **"Are not all angels ministering spirits sent to serve those who will inherit salvation?"**[127] I'll also throw in some of Peter's words when writing about the nature and manner of salvation that is found in the gospel: **"Even angels long to look into these things."**[128] These two passages teach that angels are not superior to people because they are not the benefactors of God's saving grace. God has made no provision to redeem angels back into a good relationship with him; he has only chosen to do that for humans. Because angels can never experience the gospel's power, it fills them with fascination.

The last two ways that humanity is superior to the angels can be found in the words of the Apostle Paul. In 1Corinthians 6:3, Paul makes the argument that one day, believers in Jesus will judge the angels. Angels do not judge humanity, but humanity will judge the angels. Also, in his final book of the Bible, before he is put to death, Paul, in Second Timothy 2:12, wrote these words to encourage perseverance in the faith, **"If we endure, we will also reign with him."**[129] For those who persevere in their faith, there is a promise that, in some sense, one day, we will reign with Jesus. An angel is never promised to reign with Jesus; that is a promise that is only for humanity. I find a sense of irony in that people are fascinated and long to be angels, while angels are fascinated and long to be a part of humanity because humanity is God's greatest creation.

Why is humanity God's greatest creation? The answer is that we are the only things in existence made in God's image. Regardless of what anyone believes about God, all people everywhere are created in his image. What does it exactly mean to be made in the image of God? The funny thing is that the Bible never directly states what it means to be made in God's image. From the totality of scripture, it seems the image of God is simply something we are without having to do anything. At the same time, being made in God's image seems like it comes with certain responsibilities in order to experience what it means to be made in his image.

In Genesis 2:15 it says, **"The LORD God took the man and put him in the Garden of Eden to work it and take care of it."**[130] During his work on Genesis, John H. Sailhamer, who at one time served as the professor of Old Testament studies at Golden Gate Baptist Theological Seminary, came to a very unique conclusion on how Genesis 2:15 should be translated. Through his studies of the Hebrew language, Sailhamer determined that Genesis 2:15 should be read as

"The LORD God took the man and put him in the Garden of Eden to worship and obey."[131] With this translation of Genesis 2:15, one of the main ways we display that we are an image-bearer of God is through worship.

One of the most impactful worship experiences that I have ever been a part of did not take place at a church. One of the biggest worship experiences that I have ever attended took place at Beaver Stadium, home of the Nittany Lions, We Are Penn State! If you are a fan of any Ohio-based team, please feel free to put this book down for a moment and get right with Jesus, then return to this book once you know how to cheer for a proper football team. Now that you are back, let me tell you that the Penn State football game was nothing short of a worship experience. There was chanting, there was music, there was the adoration of the crowd, and there was even a mascot doing flips throughout the game. We all know church would be more exciting if there were a mascot doing flips during the time of praise and worship! In all seriousness, though, I am trying to make the point that, as people, we are created to worship.

At this point, you might be wondering what exactly worship is. Since there is not one definition for worship, let me humbly say that for our sakes, in reading this book, worship is defined as whatever we shape our lives around. For some of us, that could be family, sports, a job, grades, etc. All the things that I have just listed are not wrong in themselves, but they become wrong when they take the place of God in shaping our lives. John Calvin once famously concluded, "The human heart is a perpetual idol factory."[132] As humans, we have an innate desire for worship. Whatever we worship shapes our lives. As image bearers of God, we need to shape our lives around him. The most heartbreaking stories I come across do not come from people who have chased a dream and failed. No, the most heartbreaking stories I come across are from people who have chased a dream and fulfilled that dream but still remain empty. These people have unfortunately discovered the same truth as King Solomon once did when he wrote that a life not shaped around God is "'**Meaningless! Meaningless!' says the teacher. 'Utterly meaningless! Everything is meaningless.'**"[133] What or who is shaping your life?

How is God best worshiped? To answer this question, the Westminster Shorter Catechism says, "Man's chief end is to glorify God and to enjoy him forever." God desires to be glorified. To glorify is to make much of, or another way of saying this is that we glorify God when we give him the proper respect, love, and honor he deserves. When it comes to the Garden of Eden, some people make the common mistake that it was God's desire for humanity to be in the garden forever. However, in a conversation God has with Adam and Eve, part of Genesis 1:28 says, "**God blessed them and said to them, 'Be fruitful and increase in number; fill the earth....**" It was never God's desire for Adam and Eve and their descendants to remain forever in Eden. God told Adam and Eve to fill the earth so that his image would be displayed all over the planet. This is why, at the end of the gospel of Matthew, in his final conversation with his disciples, Jesus tells them, "**All authority in heaven and on earth has been given to me. Therefore go and make disciples of all nations, baptizing them in the name of the Father, and of the Son, of the Holy Spirit, and teaching them to obey everything I have commanded you. And surely I am with you always, to the very end of the age.**"[134] God's glory is displayed when people have their lives shaped around him. Jesus desires that people worship and obey him, as originally stated from the very beginning in Genesis 2:15. People worship God when they are followers of Jesus Christ. G.K. Beale and Mitchell Kim are correct when they declare, "...Worship is the fuel of mission, for worshippers bear and reflect the image of God, and worship is the goal of mission, as those images are multiplied to fill the earth with divine glory."[135] As image bearers of God, we display his image when we are active in spreading his image through evangelism and discipleship of others.

When it comes to an understanding of what it means to be made in the image of God, Beale and Kim share an important insight within the context of how the ancient world would have understood being made in the image of God by writing, "In the ancient Near East, gods frequently established kings as their images in a land to express their authority (even though these kings were images of false gods). Adam was created in the image of the triune God to indicate his presence and rule over the earth. As God's image, Adam and Eve were to reign with God as kings and representatives of God."[136] With this in mind, we have a better understanding of Genesis 1:26, **"[26]Then God said, 'Let us make mankind in our image, in our likeness, so that they may rule over the fish in the sea and the birds in the sky, over the livestock and all the wild animals, and over all the creatures that move along the ground."[137]** We see this same concept repeated in Psalm 8:6-8, **"[6]You made them rulers over the works of your hands; you put everything under their feet: [7]all flocks and herds, and the animals of the wild, [8]the birds in the sky, and the fish in the sea, all that swim the paths of the sea."[138]** As we can tell from the insights of Beale and Kim, Genesis 1:26, and Psalm 8:6-8, a part of being made in God's image is to exhibit dominion.

What an image we are getting of what it means to be a part of humanity. You, I and all of the human race were meant to be kings and queens ruling over creation under the authority of the kingship of God. The question that should come to mind is, what does dominion look like in our lives today? This question is especially important for those who are like me and REALLY aren't fans of wildlife. Actually, I kid you not. There was one time in my life when I was held hostage in my car by a friend's pet turkey for a solid fifteen to thirty minutes.....but that is a story for another time. Back to the question at hand, though, for us to display dominion today is to practice proper stewardship. Stewardship is the idea of taking proper care of the things God has entrusted us. Whatever blessings God has placed in our lives, we have a responsibility to treat those things or people in our lives, like our spouse or children, with the proper value God has assigned to them. In writing this, I think some of us realize we do not even display proper dominion over the state of our homes. In writing this, I realize I have dirty dishes in my sink and clothes scattered all over my bedroom. I'm going to take some time to wash my dishes and fold my clothes as you ponder or do the same thing. I'm doing this so that I feel less of a hypocrite. Okay, now that we are both back with clean rooms and kitchens, living out the principle of dominion as those made in God's image will practically play itself out in a life that reflects order and not chaos. In one sense, our world and our lives reflect a state of chaos because we fail to live out our God-given mandate of having proper dominion. What are the blessings that God has placed within your authority?

What happens when we forget that we and others are made in the image of God? Let me briefly share the story of a man named Ota Benga with you. Ota Benga was an African pygmy who spent his early years in the Congo. Benga was more than likely born in 1833. Benga was at one time married, but unfortunately, both his wife and children were killed, and Benga found himself on a slave market in 1904. It was at this time that he was discovered by Samuel Philips Verner, who at one time served as a Presbyterian minister. Verner was in the Congo because he was hired to locate pygmies and bring them to the Saint Louis World Fair. Verner purchased Benga from the slave trade and brought him to America. In an unfortunate turn of events, Benga, in September 1906, found himself living in the Bronx Zoo on exhibit in the Monkey House, living with the other monkeys that called the Monkey House their home. If you google Ota Benga, you can find pictures of him displayed in the Monkey House.

Needless to say, having Ota Benga on display at the Bronx Zoo caused all sorts of discussions. One voice that raised concerns over having Ota Benga displayed as an animal was the black Reverand James H. Gordon, who said, "We are frank enough to say we do not like this exhibition of one of our own race with the monkeys. Our race, we think, is depressed enough, without exhibiting one of us with the apes. We think we are worthy of being considered human beings, with souls."[139]

As I said, there were many voices and many opinions on the Ota Benga situation. A voice that was the polar opposite of Rev. Gordon came from an editorial in the New York Times that said, "We do not quite understand all the emotion which others are expressing in the matter…. It is absurd to make moan over the imagined humiliation and degradation Benga is suffering. The pygmies… are very low in the human scale, and the suggestion that Benga should be in a school instead of a cage ignores the high probability that school would be a place…. from which he could draw no advantage whatever. The idea that men are all much alike except as they have had or lacked opportunities for getting an education out of books is now far out of date."[140]

Ideas have consequences. The idea during the time of Ota Benga was the endorsement of evolution. With the idea of evolution being accepted, the idea that all people are created in the image of God was rejected. Remember, James H. Gordon mentioned that he wished people would see him as someone who possessed a soul. In evolution, that idea is completely rejected, and the danger becomes that some people are more evolved than others. That some people are better than others. This line of thinking is what led to Ota Benga being placed on exhibit in a zoo with monkeys because, to some people, he was not an image bearer of God but simply an animal. Ideas have consequences.

Eventually, Ota Benga was released from living in a zoo and spent some time in Lynchburg, Virginia, attending Virginia Theological Seminary and College. Ota Benga even found employment in a Tobacco Factory. However, the trauma of living in the zoo and prior heartbreaks to that experience had taken their toll on Benga. Longing to return to the Congo, he began to save money so that he could return home. Much to his dismay, though, in 1914, World War 1 broke out, and all passenger ships from the U.S. and the Congo came to an end. In his depression that he might possibly never see his homeland ever again, Ota Benga, at the age of 32 in 1916, shot himself in the heart, taking his own life.

From Ota Benga's horrific life, we learn this sobering lesson: all the greatest injustices that take place on our planet happen because somewhere along the line, someone quit viewing people as image bearers of God and instead viewed them as something lower. The greatest tragedies that will occur in your life will come from the fact that you do not view yourself primarily as someone made in the image of God. Whatever the theology or doctrine we have about people, we cannot forget that people are special because they are made in God's image. Once you forget that truth, the door is open to all sorts of horrors.

When I consider how to close this chapter, I am drawn back to an encounter that Jesus had with the religious leaders of his day. In their attempt to make Jesus fall into a trap, they asked him if paying taxes to Caesar is a good thing. We are told this from Mark 12:16-17, **"[16]They brought the coin, and he asked them, 'Whose image is this? And whose inscription?' 'Caesar's,' they replied. [17]Then Jesus said to them, 'Give back to Caesar what is Caesar's and to God what is God's.'"**[141] What I love about this event in the life of Jesus is that it all centers on image. Jesus tells those around him that if a coin is in the image of Caesar, then give the coin to Caesar. However, whatever belongs to God, Jesus says we need to give to God. I cannot stress this enough: we are made in the image of God, and we need to give ourselves over to him. When it comes to your life, your greatest satisfaction will come when you give yourself to the one in whose image you are made and reflect. Give to God what is God's.

6

Chapter 6: You Are Fallen

Nothing in the world is the way that it should be. This is a thought that often comes to my mind. Many people object to Christianity because they point to the world's condition and wonder why a good God would allow the world to exist the way that it does. One of the most significant arguments against Christianity is the problem of evil. If you have ever taken a philosophy course or ever had a debate about the character of God, then you are more than familiar with the argument from the ancient philosopher Epicurus, who argued, "Is God willing to prevent evil, but not able? Then he is not all-powerful. Is he able, but not willing? Then he is evil. Is he both able and willing? Then whence cometh evil? Is he neither able nor willing? Then why call him God?"[142] The problem of evil is an issue that some of God's greatest servants struggled with, such as Habakkuk, who wailed, **"How long, O LORD, must I call for help? But you do not listen! Violence is everywhere! But you do not come to save. Must I forever see these evil deeds? Why must I watch all this misery?**[143] How do we make sense of the world we live in, and what role do we play in the world's problems, if any?

To answer the question about evil in our world, we need to look at what answers Genesis has for us. When Moses wrote Genesis, we

63

need to remember that Moses was writing to the Israelites who lived in a society bombarded with rival gods and rival creation stories that competed for the hearts of the Israelites.[144] In writing Genesis, Moses attempted to answer the questions of the origin of the world, humanity, and why the world is the way it is so that his fellow countrymen could make sense of it. Let's see what Moses gives us to help us understand the world and its current condition.

If you have read Genesis chapters 1 and 2, you might wonder why Genesis repeats the narrative of the creation of man and woman. The reason for this is that it all goes back to revealing the character of God. In Genesis chapter 1, God is referred to only as God. However, the Hebrew word for God is Elohim and carries behind it the idea that God is all-powerful and that he is all supreme. God is powerful enough to speak the universe in existence. In Genesis chapter 2, the word LORD comes before God. When you see LORD in the Bible, it refers to God as Yahweh. Yahweh is the personal name of God. Genesis chapter 2 stresses that God is all-powerful and supreme; he is also the God who desires to be personal with his creation. How personal is God? Well in Genesis 2, God does not speak man into existence like he does every-thing else, but he takes time to form man out of the dust and to breathe life into the first man, Adam. Then God forms Eve out of Adam's rib and brings Eve to Adam so that the first family can be formed.

So far, everything seems to be heading in the right direction, so what went wrong? In Genesis chapter 3, we are told that the serpent, who in actuality is Satan, tempts Adam and Eve to disobey God by eating the fruit from the tree of the knowledge of good and evil. At this point, you might be asking the question, how did Satan end up in Eden? To be perfectly honest with you, nobody knows for sure the origin of Satan. Many people, however, point to Isaiah 14:12-15 and Ezekiel 28:11-19 as the origins of the devil. What we do know is that Jesus compares Satan falling from heaven to a lightning bolt hitting the earth in Luke chapter 10. At this point, I think the insights of Pastor John P. Burke would do us well, who wrote, "Finally, though the Bible has little to say about Satan's origin, it does spell out his ultimate and final destiny.

Jesus said in Matthew 25:41 that hell was being prepared for 'the devil and his angels.' Beyond these facts, perhaps we dare not speculate."[145] It would seem from a biblical point of view that understanding the sin origins of Satan and his angels is not as vital for us to understand the current makeup of our world as it is to understand the origin of sin as it relates to Adam and Eve.

Getting back to the temptation of Adam and Eve, Satan lures them away from God by having a conversation with Eve while Adam observes with Satan, saying, **"Did God really say, 'You must not eat from any tree in the garden'? The woman said to the serpent, 'We may eat fruit from the trees in the garden, but God did say, 'You must not eat fruit from the tree that is in the middle of the garden, and you must not touch it, or you will die."** [146] Remember that in chapter 2, God is referred to as LORD God because God is personal. Satan does not have an intimate relationship with God; he recognizes God as all-powerful, but it stops there for Satan when it comes to God. To bring Eve into temptation, he never says LORD God; he only says God and Eve responds to Satan by referring to God as Satan does. Adam and Eve began their descent into sin, as we all do, by failing to recognize the character of God. You can view God as powerful all you want, but if you do not see him also as a God that wants to be invested in your life, what good is it if he is powerful? The door to sin is open when we fail to see that God is not only all-powerful, but that he also strongly desires a relationship with us. My question for you when it comes to God isn't if you view him as omnipotent; my question for you is, do you think he wants a cherished relationship with you?

Picking up on the conversation between Satan and Eve, Genesis 3:4-7 says, **"4 'You will not certainly die,' the serpent said to the woman. 5 'For God knows that when you eat from it your eyes will be opened, and you will be like God, knowing good and evil.' 6 When the woman saw that the tree was good for food and pleasing to the eye, and also desirable for gaining wisdom, she took some and ate it. She also gave some to her husband, who**

was with her, and he ate it. ⁷Then the eyes of both of them were opened, and they realized they were naked; so they sewed fig leaves together and made coverings for themselves." This is where everything goes wrong. Adam and Eve trusted the lies of Satan more than the trustworthiness of God. Satan told Adam and Eve that God was holding out on them. That God was not giving his best to them. That if they wanted to experience the best of life, they needed to do it on their own terms. By trusting Satan over God, a great tragedy was jumpstarted. This tragedy is so great that it is referred to as The Fall.

As soon as Adam and Eve ate the forbidden fruit, it is recorded that they felt shame at being naked. All they could do to cover up their shame was to sew fig leaves in an attempt to conceal their embarrassment. In their attempt to become God's equal in knowledge, Adam and Eve ultimately did not find the wisdom they sought, but in its place, they found guilt, shame, and inner turmoil. Also, when God showed up in the garden, we are told that Adam and Eve tried to hide from him. In response to their hiding, we are told in verse 9, **"Then the LORD God called to the man, 'Where are you?'"**[147] If God is all-knowing as the bible states, then why did he ask Adam where was he? The reason for this is that God wanted Adam to be fully aware of the weightiness of everything that was taking place. God wanted Adam to know what type of world he was living in now.

God, being the righteous judge, brought judgment against those who violated his law. Even though God brought judgment in his judgments, he also extended mercy. We see this mercy because when he talks to the serpent, he says, **"And I will put enmity between you and the woman, and between your offspring and hers; he will crush your head, and you will strike his heel."**[148] What we have here is called the Protoevangelium, or otherwise known as the first gospel. In Genesis 3:15, God is saying that one day sinful humanity will be redeemed because Jesus will come. Satan might bruise Jesus, but Jesus will have the ultimate victory by crushing him. The hope here is that God does not abandon his people to darkness but makes a way for them to return to him. Next, God tells Eve, **"I will make your pains in childbearing very severe; with painful labor you will give birth to children. Your desire will be for your husband, and he will rule over you."**[149] What we see here is that God tells Eve giving birth will be a painful process, but the blessing is that she will still have children and will be able to raise a family. God also mentions that Eve will now have conflict in her marriage with Adam. The nature of the conflict will be the issue of submission, and we see this issue play out in numerous marriages today. Something that needs to be stated is that when we discuss submission, it must always go back to the trinity. Within the trinity, we see Jesus always submitting to God the Father. Even before the Fall, Eve was meant to submit to Adam, but due to the Fall, submission will be difficult for wives. God, knowing of this difficulty, gives this advice in Ephesians 5:22-25, **"[22]Wives, submit yourselves to your own husbands as you do to the Lord. [23]For the husband is the head of the wife as Christ is the head of the church, his body, of which he is the Savior. [24]Now as the church submits to Christ, so also wives should submit to their husbands in everything. [25]Husbands, love your wives as Christ loved the church and gave himself up for her."**[150]

As we see here, wives are called to submit to their husbands, but husbands are called to love their wives as Christ loved the church. More wives might be willing to submit if more husbands were willing to love their wives as Jesus loves his church. In speaking about men turning back to the consequences that God passes out, he told Adam, **"Cursed is the ground because of you; through painful toil you will eat food from it all the days of your life. It will produce thorns and thistles for you, and you will eat the plants of the field. By the sweat of your brow you will eat your food until you return to the ground, since from it you were taken; for dust you are and to dust you will return."**[151] With Adam, God tells him that the world he will now live in will be one in which he can find success, but it will be difficult to achieve, and he will struggle to live in it. God also tells Adam that eventually, the strength of his body will fail and that death will come for him. The punishments that God gave to Adam and Eve are punishments that we, as their descendants, experience today and see all around us.

You might be thinking at this point, why do we have to suffer for the sin that Adam committed? Well for starters, Paul in Romans 5:12 wrote, **"Therefore, just as sin entered the world through one man, and death through sin, and in this way death came to all people, because all sinned."**[152] Later in the same chapter, in verse 19, Paul also wrote, **"For just as through the disobedience of the one man the many were made sinners...."**[153] This is interesting because if you remember, Satan sinned prior to Adam and Eve, and yet his sin did not impact the status of humanity. However, due to Adam, Paul makes the argument that his sin affects all of us; why is that the case? Also, why isn't Eve mentioned by Paul since she was the one who gave the fruit to him? The reason for this is that Adam acted as a representative for all humanity, and as humanity's representative, when he sinned, all of humanity became guilty and inherited his sin as well. This is known as original sin.

The impact of Adam's sin and the viability of original sin has sparked heated discussions amongst people for centuries. The reason for this is because at the heart of original sin is getting at what is the nature of mankind. Are people inherently good, or are people inherently bad? The Bible has quite a peculiar take on human nature, on the one hand stating that all people are made in the image of God, but on the other arguing that due to sin, human nature is inherently flawed. One way to think about this is like pineapple on a pizza. You see, pizza is one of the best foods out there but if you put pineapple on it, it is now flawed. In fact, there is a rare chance that you might even like pineapple on a pizza, and this only confirms that human nature is flawed!

In trying to understand human nature, Solomon wrote in Ecclesiastes 7:29, **"This only have I discovered: God made humankind upright, but they have sought many evil schemes."**[154] Alan Jacobs in *Original Sin* wrote in regards to this doctrine, "Again and again the literature and culture of the West have returned to this doctrine, worrying over it, loathing it, rejecting it-only to call it back in times of great crisis or great misery."[155] Even though people might try to run from the idea of original sin, it is hard to deny. A well-known opponent of Christianity, Sigmund Freud, on lamenting what he saw in human nature, once wrote, "Men are not gentle, friendly creatures wishing for love, who simply defend themselves if they are attacked, but that a powerful measure of desire for aggression has to be reckoned as part of their instinctual endowment.……*Homo homini lupus* [man is a wolf]; who has the courage to dispute it in the face of all the evidence in his own life and in history."[156]

When does our sin nature start to impact us? David, in trying to make sense of his nature after he sent Uriah, one of his loyal soldiers, to death so that Uriah would not find out that David fathered a child with Bathsheba, who was the wife of Uriah wrote, **"Surely I was sinful at birth, sinful from the time my mother conceived me."** In a conversation with Noah after the events of the flood, God told him, **"Never again will I curse the ground because of humans, even though every inclination of the human heart is evil from childhood."**[157] From our very conception in our mother's wombs, our sin nature is present within us, and according to God, even as children, our hearts are full of evil due to sin.

Before sin is ever an outward action, it takes place within our hearts, and, according to God, our hearts are evil. At this point, you might have the desire to push back against the idea that our hearts are evil. You might even want to point to the genuine good in the world that people do, to say we are not as bad as I am making us out to be. With that train of thought, let's take a look at a time when Jesus encouraged people to pray. In Matthew 7:9-11 Jesus said, **"⁹Which of**

you, if your son asks for bread will give him a stone? [10]Or if he asks for a fish will give him a snake? [11]If you, then, though you are evil, know how to give good gifts to your children, how much more will your Father in heaven give good gifts to those who ask him!"[158] Even though we are evil, according to Jesus, we still possess the capacity to do good things. This is because people are still made in the image of God, even if that image is marred by sin. Paul in Romans even goes so far as to say that God has written his law into our hearts so that we know what is right from wrong. The issue isn't that we do not know the difference between right and wrong; it is that even though we know the right things to do, we willfully choose the wrong. As Erickson puts it, "Further, many people are unable to grasp the concept of sin. The idea of sin as an inner force, an inherent condition, a controlling power, is largely unknown....it is not simply we are sinners because we sin; we sin because we are sinners."[159]

At this point, we can hopefully agree that the condition of our world is less than ideal. Many people who have gone through intense heartache and suffering beg the question, why doesn't God instantly make things right? As Christians, we believe that God is all-powerful and that in his power, he can instantly correct the evil in our world. The question we must try to answer is why God allows the world to continue as it is. One answer to this question is that God is infuriatingly kind. In 2Kings 21:1-18 and 2Chronicles 32:33-33:20, we have the life recap of King Manasseh. What do we know about King Manasseh? Well, for starters, he reigned as king for fifty-five years and became king at twelve. I do not know about you, but I know twelve-year-olds I wouldn't trust watching over my pet, let alone wanting them to rule over a kingdom. If you guessed that Manasseh was a horrible king, then you guessed correctly. 2 Kings 21:2-6 says, **"[2]He did evil in the eyes of the LORD, following the detestable practices of the nations the LORD had driven out before the Israelites. [3]He rebuilt the high places his father Hezekiah had destroyed; he also erected altars to Baal and made an Asherah pole, as Ahab king** of Israel had done. He bowed down to all the starry hosts and worshiped them. **⁴He built altars in the temple of the LORD, of which the LORD had said, 'In Jerusalem I will put my Name.' ⁵In the two courts of the temple of the LORD, he built altars to all the starry hosts. ⁶He sacrificed his own son in the fire, practiced divination, sought omens, and consulted mediums and spirits. He did much evil in the eyes of the LORD, arousing his anger."**[160] The rest of 2 Kings, when it refers to Manasseh, mentions that God will punish the nation because of him, and then we are told that he died and was buried with his ancestors.

In 2 Chronicles, we get pretty much a rehash of the deeds of Manasseh. However, we get to see the punishment that God brought to Manasseh in 2ⁿᵈ Chronicles 33:10-11 that says, **"¹⁰The LORD spoke to Manasseh and his people, but they paid no attention. ¹¹So the LORD brought against them the army commanders of the king of Assyria, who took Manasseh prisoner, put a hook in his nose, bound him with bronze shackles and took him to Babylon."**[161] So far, everything is lining up the way I would expect it for Manasseh, who is a wicked king who led an entire nation away from God, and not only that, let's not forget that he even took one of his own children and sacrificed him by burning him alive. However, verses 12-13 record something shocking, **"¹²But while in deep distress, Manasseh sought the LORD his God and sincerely humbled himself before the God of his ancestors. ¹³And when he prayed, the LORD listened to him and was moved by his request. So the LORD brought Manasseh back to Jerusalem and to his kingdom. Then Manasseh finally realized that the LORD alone is God!"**[162] Manasseh prayed to God while he was rightfully under God's judgment. We are told God was so moved by Manasseh's prayer that God quit punishing him and brought him back to his own kingdom. Manasseh, one of the worst kings in Israel's history, due to the kindness of God, had a change of heart and would dedicate the rest of his life to undoing the evil he had done in his younger years.

Maybe you are like me and are wondering why there are two different accounts of Manasseh's life. Why did the book of Kings not include the change of heart that Manasseh goes through, as Chronicles shows? To answer this question, we go back to the respective purposes of the Kings and Chronicles. First and Second Kings was written during a time in which Israel found itself living in captivity with their nation destroyed by Babylon. First and Second Kings is answering the question "Why did God punish us?" The answer being, God punished Israel due to its persistent rebellion against him.[163] First and Second Chronicles was written at the end of Israel's captivity in Babylon and their return back to their homeland. First and Second Chronicles is reaffirming the truth that even though God punishes his people, he still deeply loves them and does not abandon them forever. In both Kings and Chronicles, Manasseh is a key figure. In Kings, he shows why Israel deserved punishment, and Chronicles Manasseh is a great example of showing God's kindness to those not deserving of it. If God is willing to be kind to Manasseh, will he not also extend that same kindness to you as well? Why does God allow evil to continue in our world and not punish it immediately? In the life of Manasseh we see that the God that punishes sinners is the same God that graciously welcomes sinners to experience his infinite kindness.

Even though God is kind and patient, that does not make living in the world easy. In fact, if I am honest, the kindness and patience of God, and I mean this with all the reverence I can muster, it just sucks at times. When it comes to heartache and realizing how hard life can be at times, Job stands head and shoulders above most. If you are not familiar with Job, he is a righteous man that Satan wants to cause to fall, and God allows Satan to tempt Job to see if Job will turn his back on God and renounce his faith. In a series of repeated heartbreaks, Job loses his wealth, health, and all his children. Later on, Job is visited by his friends, and after a while, they accuse Job of having done something wrong for his life to play out the way that it has. Job, like anyone in his situation, finds himself asking question after question after question on why God would allow him to suffer the way that he is. God eventually shows up, and he does not answer any of Job's questions about how he runs the world. Instead, he begins to question Job about his knowledge of the world. At one point in his questioning of Job, God brings up two creatures called leviathan and behemoth.

Much has been written about these two creatures, trying to figure out their identity, with some even suggesting that God is referring to some type of dinosaur-like animals. The identity of the leviathan and behemoth is not what concerns us in this chapter. However, I bet they would be amazing creatures to see. It would be an amazing experience to see these two animals, but I am sure they would not be safe to be around. That is the point that God is making to Job, that the world's current condition is that our world can be an amazing place to live, but it will not always be safe. The world is not as it should be, but it is still one in which God can be found. Job, in the midst of unimaginable suffering, was still able to find God. Even though the world is far from ideal it is still a world that declares the glory of God. When we look at the condition of the world and ponder its current condition, I think it is best to look to the wisdom of G.K. Chesterton. For those unfamiliar with Chesterton, he was an English writer, philosopher, apologist, theologian, and a literary and art critic who lived early in the 20th century. In responding to a news article that said the world's problems could be fixed through economics and government reform, Chesterton responded, "In one sense, and the eternal sense, the thing is plain. The answer to the question 'What is wrong?' is, or should be, 'I am wrong.' Until a man can give that answer his idealism is only a hobby."[164] What is wrong with our world? Why is our world the way that it is? The answer to why the world is not functioning as it should, as Chesterton reminds us, is that we are not functioning as we should. That human nature is fallen, and because we are fallen we have a fallen world.

7
───

Chapter 7: You Are Redeemed

Have you ever had the unpleasant experience of falling for a scam? In my early twenties, I was in a Barnes & Noble, minding my own business, when a man in a suit walked up to me and told me he had locked his keys in a car and needed help. This man gave me a sob story about needing to call a locksmith to help him get into his car but had no money to pay for help. Like a fool, I offered him a ride in my car, took him to the closest ATM, and withdrew a decent amount of money to help this individual out. Once we arrived back at Barnes & Noble, this man couldn't thank me enough for my generosity, and I went back into the store as he waited in the parking lot. Once in the store, however, I looked out the window, and much to my surprise, this man, this wolf in sheep's clothing, pulled out of his pocket another set of keys and unlocked the door to his car. In much righteous indignation, I rushed out of the store to confront the man as he was entering his car. I want to tell you that I got my money back. I want to tell you that this man apologized, but if you read the last chapter, you know we live in a fallen world. The man drove away in his car with a weightier wallet and left me feeling like the biggest moron on the planet. I was completely scammed.

Sometimes, it seems like a scam when I think of being saved or redeemed. What I mean by this is that it feels like, at times, as Christians, we overpromise what it feels like to be saved. How many times have you heard someone who means well say something in the vein of the following: "Once you come to Jesus, all the burdens of your heart will melt away", or "Once you accept Jesus, everything will make sense in your life", or "Once you trust Jesus your sin struggles will go away", or my all-time favorite "When you trust Jesus you'll never feel alone again." If you have been a Christian for a significant amount of time, you realize just how empty all of the above promises are, and you wouldn't be alone in this experience.

Joel Robbins, in his book *Becoming Sinners,* dives into the impact of how embracing Christianity has affected the Urapmin, a tribe that lives in Papua New Guinea. The fascinating thing about the Urapmin is that only about 400 individuals make up the tribe and each one has professed faith in Christ. The reason for this goes back to a revival that broke out amongst the Urapmin in the 1970's. Initially, with the tribe's conversion to Christianity, there was much joy and excitement, but later on, the Urapmin realized they still had the tendency to gossip about one another, they had the tendency to still lie to one another, they even still occasionally stole from one another. It wasn't for a lack of knowledge of the commandments of God, it was simply that the Urapmin chose to follow their own desires instead of God. As the Urapmin struggled with sin and tried to grow closer to God, they found more darkness and more of a desire to disobey the God they claimed to love.

I'm sure if he had had the chance, Paul would have loved to commiserate with the Urapmin. In an honest confession, Paul wrote in Romans 7:21-25, **"²¹I have discovered this principle of life—that when I want to do what is right, I inevitably do what is wrong. ²²I love God's law with all my heart. ²³But there is another power within me that is at war with my mind. This power makes me a slave to the sin that is still within me. ²⁴Oh, what a miserable person I am! Who will free me from this life that is dominated**

by sin and death? ²⁵Thank God! The answer is in Jesus Christ our Lord. So you see how it is: In my mind I really want to obey God's law, but because of my sinful nature I am a slave to sin.[165]

There are some out there who believe that Paul in these verses is talking about his life before he came to Christ and that he did not possess an intense struggle with sin once saved. However, for anyone who has tried to follow Christ, they know the truthfulness behind Paul's words. I know in my own life, in my own heart the intense battles that take place within me. I'm reminded of the words of Peter who wrote to fellow believers in 1 Peter 2:11, **"Dear friends, I urge you as foreigners and exiles, to abstain from sinful desires, which wage war against your soul."**[166] Is this really it? Is this what it means to be saved? That I have received Jesus as lord and know I am doomed to be fully aware of the sin struggles in my life until I die and go to heaven? Are we really doomed to some type of Dr. Jekyll and Mr. Hyde experience until we die? Is this what it means to be saved? Is this what it means to be redeemed?

I think in order to understand what it means to be redeemed, we need to understand what the Bible means when it declares we are saved. I guess the first thing we need to get right is what exactly we are saved from. As I have mentioned earlier, we need to be saved from the power of sin that affects us. Some people would argue that we need to be saved from the devil. I would like to present to you, however, that when the Bible warns us we need to be saved, it primarily means we need to be saved from God. As puzzling as this might be for you to read, please consider Romans 1:18, which says, **"The wrath of God is revealed from heaven against all the godlessness and wickedness of people, who suppress the truth by their wickedness."**[167] Also Ephesians 2:1-3, **"¹And you were dead in the trespasses and sins ²in which you once walked, following the course of this world, following the prince of the power of the air, the spirit that is now at work in the sons of disobedience— ³among whom we all once**

lived in the passions of our flesh, carrying out the desires of the body and the mind, and were by nature children of wrath, like the rest of mankind."[168] Finally, consider what Romans 2:4-5 says, "**⁴Or do you presume on the riches of his kindness and forbearance and patience, not knowing that God's kindness is meant to lead you to repentance? ⁵But because of your hard and impenitent heart you are storing up wrath for yourself on the day of wrath when God's righteous judgment will be revealed.**"[169]

From the above verses, we can see that the greatest need in our lives and the most significant promise of being redeemed is that we are saved from the righteous wrath of God that each one of us rightly deserves. At this point, you might be thinking that none of this makes sense, that if God is good, why does he have wrath for people? God has wrath for people because he is truly good. On this truth, C.S. Lewis had to say, "If the universe is not governed by an absolute goodness, then all our efforts are in the long run hopeless. But if it is, then we are making ourselves enemies to that goodness every day, and are not in the least likely to do any better tomorrow, and so our case is hopeless again. We cannot do without it, and we cannot do with it. God is the only comfort, He is also the supreme terror: the thing we most need and the thing we most want to hide from. He is our only possible ally, and we have made ourselves His enemies. Some people talk as if meeting the gaze of absolute goodness would be fun. They need to think again. They are only playing with religion. Goodness is either the greatest safety or the great danger – according to the way you react to it. And we have reacted the wrong way."[170]

God is the great good of the universe and because he is the great good, he cannot stand any form of injustice. The sad thing is, each of us in some way have contributed to the evil in our world and, due to that, we rightfully receive the wrath of God. The good news of the gospel, the good news of being saved, as one pastor once put it, is that we are saved "From God. By God. For God." When we look at the message of redemption, it is all God-centered. It's God-centered because the gospel begins with God and ultimately ends with God. When you think about salvation, do you see it as an event or a process? In reality, I would like to suggest that it's not either/or but both/and. In order to be saved, there has to be an event in your life when you acknowledge your need for salvation in Christ and in Christ alone. After that event has taken place in your life, the process of salvation takes place, and it takes place for the duration of your life. Once again, borrowing from the wisdom of Lewis he said, "The Christian is in a different position from other people trying to be good….He does not think God will love us because we are good, but that God will make us good because He loves us."[171] Let's take some time to see how God is in the process of making us good.

The first step in God making us good is known as justification. Being justified by God means that we are declared righteous in his sight. In other words, it means in the eyes of God we are in a good position with him. The way we become justified in the eyes of God is when we place our faith in the sacrifice of Jesus on the cross and in the hope of his resurrection. We can be declared righteous in the sight of God because God performs a great exchange on our behalf! The exchange being that while on the cross, Jesus took our sin on himself so that we can have his righteousness as 2Corinthians 5:21 says, **"God made him who had no sin to be sin for us, so that in him we might become the righteousness of God."**[172] Righteousness is not something that we can obtain ourselves as people; we will always inevitably fall short. Righteousness is something we must receive from our gracious God. As Paul reminds us in Galatians 2:21, **"I do not treat the grace of God as meaningless. For if keeping the law could make us right with God, then there was no need for Christ to die."**[173]

One man in particular who found great freedom in justification by faith alone was the German monk Martin Luther. Martin Luther is best known for being the father of the Protestant Reformation, and the story of how he kicked off the reformation is a fascinating one. The funny thing about Luther is that he never intended to become a monk but wanted a career in law. The abrupt change in career paths happened when he was 22 and traveling to a nearby village when a thunderstorm broke out. The severity of the storm was so severe, a bolt of lightning hit near him and in his distress, Luther cried out, "Saint Anne help me! I will become a monk."[174]

Luther survived the storm and, being a man of his word, became a monk. Unfortunately for Luther, living as a monk was less than desirable. The reason for this was that Luther could not shake the feeling that God was angry with him. Luther would spend hours confessing every sin he could think of in trying to seek and find God's approval. At one point Luther even said, "If I could believe that God was not angry with me, I would stand on my head for joy."[175] The more Luther tried to please God, the more he became aware of his own failures and one time while dwelling on his relationship with God, sorrowfully confessed, "Love God? Sometimes I hate him."[176]

How did Luther go from hating God to finding freedom in him? While being a monk, Luther continued his studies and eventually became a professor of theology. While going through Romans, Luther read Romans 1:16-17, "**[16]For I am not ashamed of the power of the gospel, for it is the power of God for salvation for everyone who believes, to the Jew first and also to the Greek. [17]For in it the righteousness of God is revealed from faith for faith, as it is written, 'The righteous shall live by faith.'**"[177] While studying this text and especially verse 17, Luther, in his own words, had to say, "I greatly longed to understand Paul's Epistle to the Romans, and nothing stood in the way but that one expression, 'The justice of God,' because I took it to mean that justice whereby God is just and deals justly in punishing the unjust. My situation was that, although an impeccable monk, I stood before God as a sinner troubled in conscience, and I had no confidence that my merit would assuage him. Therefore I did not love a just and angry God, but rather hated and murmured against him. Yet I clung to the dear Paul and had a great yearning to know what he meant.

Night and day I pondered until I saw the connection between the justice of God and the statement that 'the just shall live by his faith.' Then I grasped that the justice of God is that righteousness by which through grace and sheer mercy God justifies us through faith. Thereupon I felt myself to be reborn and to have gone through open doors into paradise. The whole of Scripture took on a new meaning, and whereas before the 'justice of God' had filled me with hate, now it became to me inexpressibly sweet in greater love. This passage of Paul became to me a gate to heaven....If you have a true faith that Christ is your Saviour, then at once you have a gracious God, for faith leads you in and opens up God's heart and will, that you should see pure grace and overflowing love. This it is to behold God in faith that you should look upon his fatherly, friendly heart, in which there is no anger nor ungraciousness. He who sees God as angry does not see him rightly but looks only on a curtain, as if a dark cloud had been drawn across his face." [178] Luther went from hating God to finding freedom in God because he realized that in Jesus he was redeemed by God. This promise holds true for any person who is willing to come to God.

Even though Martin Luther was the father of the Protestant Reformation, the most influential theologian of the Reformation was probably John Calvin. The reason for this is that John Calvin was the first theologian to make a distinction between justification and sanctification.[179] At this time, you might not be familiar with the term sanctification, but it is the second step in the process of salvation. In justification, we are declared righteous in the eyes of God, while at the same time in sanctification, we are being made righteous in the sight of God.

When we think about these two aspects of salvation between justification and sanctification, we should see justification as a positional standing with God and sanctification as a relational standing with God. Think of it as a parent and child relationship. No matter what happens in your relationship, your child will always be your child; that position does not change. In the same way, because of justification, we are always positionally in a good standing with God as Ephesians 2:4-6 says, "**⁴But God is so rich in mercy, and he loved us so much, ⁵that** even though we were dead because of our sins, he gave us life when he raised Christ from the dead. (It is only by God's grace that you have been saved!) ⁶For he raised us from the dead along with Christ and seated us with him in the heavenly realms because we are united with Christ Jesus."[180] From God's perspective, when he stares at us, he sees us as positionally seated with Jesus in the heavenly realm! Our position with God never changes because God has declared us righteous due to the righteousness of Jesus!

As I have already stated, from a positional standpoint, as a parent, your child is always your child, and as a child, your parent is always your parent. However, from a relational standpoint, a parent-and-child relationship might not always be what it should be. Just as a parent and child relationship might not be what it should be relationally, our relationship with God at times can be in the same boat. Sanctification is the process in which we grow to live out relationally with God what we are positionally in him.

How does God accomplish the process of sanctification in our lives? The answer is found in Ephesians 2:8-10 which says, "⁸For by grace you have been saved through faith. And this is not your own doing; it is the gift of God, ⁹not a result of works, so that no one may boast. ¹⁰For we are his workmanship, created in Christ Jesus for good works, which God prepared beforehand, that we should walk in them."[181] These three verses are my favorite in Ephesians because they are full of soul-reviving truths. Paul uses the word workmanship to describe us. If you are not familiar with the term workmanship, it carries the idea that we are a masterpiece. I do not know how you view yourself, but let me remind you that because you are redeemed in the eyes of God, he views you as an artist who takes in his work and rejoices in it. Another thing that Paul teaches us about salvation is that it is not based on our works but a gift from God. This brings us to sanctification, in which Paul tells us that we are created in Christ Jesus for good works! We grow relationally in our relationship with God by accomplishing the good works that he has for us. The wonderful thing about these good works is that God has had them planned for us long before we ever came to him for salvation.

I wonder if you are reading this book, do you have a driver's license? If so, I wonder if you can recall what it was like for you to have to get your license? Like most things in my life, it became an ordeal. When it came to me getting my license, I didn't receive it until my third attempt at the test. Honestly, in the story I am about to tell you, I probably shouldn't have received it until at least my sixth attempt! Fresh off getting my license, I was asked to drop off a relative at my grandparents' home. I was an eager young driver with the road as my playground! I drove perfectly to my destination, but unfortunately, I had to park my car, and this is where everything fell apart, literally! You see, I wanted to park my car as close to the curb as possible, and I took out my grandparents' mailbox! I know you are probably picturing that it all happened in one swift motion, but in reality, it was all too painfully slow! I don't know why I did this, but as I was hitting the mailbox and knew it was falling from its hinges, I kept driving forward as the poor mailbox held on for dear life. By the time I realized everything that was taking place and I stopped the car, the mailbox was hanging by its hinges in such a way that it was swaying back and forth as if shaking with disapproval at the whole ordeal. To add to this chaos of a situation, my grandad had been observing the entire catastrophe by looking through the screen door, burst through the door with all the grace of an eighty-year-old man, and ran to his mailbox. As he consoled his mailbox in his hands, he looked at me with a fit of rage and laid into me with words that are not appropriate to put in print, and probably also not appropriate for me to dwell on either!

Why do I bring all this up about a car? Well, as one professor once told me, salvation is like receiving a car as a gift. The car is a gift that is freely given to us, but it comes with responsibilities such as paying for gas, insurance, and overall maintenance of the vehicle. In the same way God tells us that salvation is a gift that he freely gives to us, but with that gift comes the responsibilities of doing the good works that God has prepared for us to accomplish. I do not know about you, but for me, at times the Christian life is a rewarding life, but it is also a difficult life as well. There are times in which I always do not know what good works God wants me to accomplish. There are other times in which I am pretty sure of what God wants from me, but it seems completely overwhelming. When this happens, I turn to Romans 8:34 for comfort and I hope you find comfort in these words as well, **"Who then will condemn us? No one—for Christ Jesus died for us, and was raised to life for us, and he is sitting in the place of honor at God's right hand, pleading for us."**[182] When we feel like we are condemned, when we feel overwhelmed by life, Paul reminds us that Jesus is at the right hand of his father praying on our behalf. Robert Murray M'Cheyne was a minister in the Church of Scotland and, while pondering on the truth that Jesus prayed for him, said, "If I could hear Christ praying for me in the next room, I would not fear a million enemies. Yet distance makes no difference. He is praying for me."[183] As you seek to become relationally what you are positionally in God, know Jesus is praying precisely that for you in your spiritual growth.

Regarding the transformative power of sanctification, I want to share the story of John Newton with you. For those not familiar with John Newton, he wrote the hymn "Amazing Grace", and his story is a story of how God's amazing grace can shape one's life. Newton was raised by his father, a ship's captain, and his mother, a devout Christian. When it came to his spiritual formation, John's mother was the sole one responsible for that. However, in a tragic turn of events, Newton would lose his mother at the age of seven when she would die from tuberculosis, and his spiritual interests died with her. Newton's father would remarry, but sadly, Newton did not connect with his step-mother. When it came to his father, he described his father as having a desire to distance himself from him.

At age eleven he would join his father in the family business of sailing. By age 18, Newton would find himself having a short stint being employed by the British navy but, due to his unruly behavior, found himself relieved from his duties and, in his own words, would say that he possessed the ambition of Caesar to rank in wickedness. With his discharge from the navy, Newton would find employment by working for ships that were a part of the African slave trade. He found the work to be an "easy and creditable way of life." Newton would work for several slave ships and eventually rose to the rank of captain of his own slave ship.

In March 1748, while asleep in the cabin of his ship, a violent storm broke out on the sea, and due to the storm's fury, a large burst of water came through the wall of his room and woke him up. Throughout the night, Newton found himself pumping water from the ship's deck in a hope to keep the ship from going under. Some of his crew lost their lives due to the events of the storm, but Newton himself survived and, at one point amidst the storm, found himself crying out to God, "Lord, have mercy."[184] Newton would say this prayer was his coming back to the faith of his childhood and that, each year for the rest of his life, he would observe the date on which he called out to God to rescue him.

The puzzling thing when it comes to John Newton is that even after being redeemed by God, he continued being a slave trader. The reason why he abandoned the slave trade was that in 1754, he suffered a seizure and had to abandon a career at sea.[185] Upon abandoning his life as a sailor, Newton eventually became a pastor in which he faithfully preached the message of the gospel to those who attended his church. The more Newton preached the gospel and grew to understand the heart of God, the more ashamed he became of his time as a slave trader and repented for his participation in slavery. For the final 19 years of his life, John Newton would speak out against slavery, hoping to see it come to an end in Great Britain. In his efforts to fight against slavery, he would write *Thoughts Upon The African Slave Trade*. He would say, "I am bound, in conscience, to take shame to myself by a public confession, which, however sincere, comes too late to prevent, or repair, the misery and mischief to which I have, formerly, been accessary....I hope it will always be a subject of humiliating reflection to me, that I was, once, an active instrument, in a business at which my heart now shudders."[186] Nine months before his death, parliament would pass a bill in which slavery was illegal in Great Britain, and much of the reason for that bill passing was due to the efforts of John Newton. In reflecting on his life, John Newton would famously say, "Although my memory's fading, I remember two things very clearly: I am a great sinner and Christ is a great Savior."[187]

In John Newton's life, we see the beauty of salvation at work, which is both an event and a process. Through sanctification, we see that salvation is not defined by who we are today but who we are becoming tomorrow, the day after tomorrow, and the day after that. John Newton, the raging racist, was saved by God, and over time, God changed Newton's heart to reflect his very own. This is the hope that you and I have as well, that the more time we spend with God, the more that he will change us as Romans 8:28-30 promises, **"[28]And we know that in all things God works for the good of those who love him, who have been called according to his purpose. [29]For those God foreknew he also predestined to be conformed to the image of his Son, that he might be the firstborn among many brothers and sisters. [30]And those he predestined, he also called; those he called, he also justified; those he justified, he also glorified.**[188] By saving you, God has a good plan for your life, and that good plan is that God is shaping us to look like Jesus more and more. As verse 30 tells us, one day, God will glorify us, which is our third and final step in the salvation process!

When it comes to glorification, even though it is the final process of salvation, unfortunately, compared to justification and sanctification, there is very little written about it. So little is written about this final step in the salvation process because there is much mystery as to what glorification will look like. Even though there is a great deal of mystery when it comes to glorification, Paul tells us in Romans 8:18, **"I consider that our present sufferings are not worth comparing with the glory that will be revealed in us."**[189] Paul admits that life is hard, but he also gives hope that the things God has in store for us will make everything worth it! According to Paul, everything we have gone through in life will be worth it because of the promise of glorification.

When does glorification take place? You see, there isn't much agreement here, but for the purpose of this book, I believe glorification will take place in two parts. One part takes place immediately when we die, while the other part will not occur until Jesus's second coming. Let's talk about the immediate part of glorification first, which is the redeeming of our very nature. Salvation promises that God corrects the inner flaws within our character.

At this point, I want to mention something I think deserves addressing. The Bible has a lot to say about the heart. In the last chapter, we discussed how our hearts are evil even from childhood. If you have been a part of any youth group, you have heard the dangers of following your heart because of Jeremiah 17:9, which says, **"The heart is deceitful above all things, and desperately sick; who can understand it?"**[190] Even though there are numerous warnings in scripture when discussing the heart, we also have to keep the words of Jesus in mind, such as when he said, **"Love the Lord your God with all your heart and with all your soul and with all your mind."**[191] Also, let us not forget Psalm 37:4, which says, **"Delight yourself in the LORD, and he will give you the desires of your heart."**[192] How do we make sense of these verses? Why would God call us to love him with a wicked heart, and why would God give us the desires of our hearts if it is wicked? The answer is that God needs to provide us with a new heart as Ezekiel 36:26-27 says, **"**[26]**AndI will give you a new heart, and I will put a new spirit in you. I will take out your stony and stubborn heart and give you a tender, responsive heart.** [27]**And I will put my Spirit in you so that you will follow my decrees and be careful to obey my regulations.**[193] God gives us a new heart as a believer; with this new heart, we desire to live for and please him. I mentioned earlier that our hearts are evil because the Bible states that, but on the flip side, it also states that as believers, God gives us a heart that desires him. So I will say this: if you are following and loving Jesus, it is okay to follow your heart; however, make sure as you follow the desires of your heart, that you are first following and obeying Jesus. Even though God has given us new hearts, and as much as I desire to follow after God, there are flaws within me that derail my walk with him. Whether it is my anger, my lust, my desire for revenge, all these qualities that are very much in me hamper me spiritually. The promise of glorification is that when we take our last breath here on earth, and when we take our first breath in heaven, God will fully redeem our souls, and that process which began when we first trusted Christ as Savior to redeem our souls will be complete.

We are told throughout the Bible that to be absent from the body is to be present with the Lord. Our loved ones who have preceded us in death are in Heaven and in the presence of God. As good as this sounds, they are in an incomplete state. How can I say that our loved ones who are experiencing the joys of heaven are in an imperfect condition? The reason why I can boldly state this is that when God created mankind, he created humanity to be a soul and body creation. God never intended for humans to have their soul and body separated; God always intended for people to have their souls and bodies united. The joy of glorification is that God will give us a new body on the day Jesus returns.

Nobody writes more about the joy of having a new body than Paul. Paul tells us, **"And if the Spirit of him who raised Jesus from the dead is living in you, he who raised Christ from the dead will also give life to your mortal bodies because of his Spirit who lives in you."**[194] In another place in Scripture Paul wrote, **"But our citizenship is in heaven. And we eagerly await a Savior from there, the Lord Jesus Christ, who by the power that enables him to bring everything under his control, will transform our lowly bodies so that they will be like his glorious body."**[195]

I've only given you a sample of what Paul writes about when it comes to God redeeming our physical bodies. However, we should consider why Paul writes so much about receiving a redeemed physical body from God. I think the answer for us can be found in 2 Corinthians 12:7-8. Here Paul shares this, "**⁷......I was given a thorn in my flesh, a messenger of Satan, to torment me. ⁸Three times I pleaded with the Lord to take it away from me.**"[196] There have been many suggestions as to what Paul's thorn in the flesh was, but the most likely answer, as David Woodall proposes, is that it was probably some recurring physical ailment that troubled Paul.[197] Whatever problem Paul had with his body, he compared it to a messenger of Satan and begged Jesus three times to remove his physical problem. I think it's important to point out that, even though Paul was a man of faith, that didn't guarantee that Jesus would answer his prayer the way he desired. Sometimes when we pray and Jesus does not respond the way we hope, it does not mean that there is something wrong with our faith. Sometimes, it means Jesus has a different plan. I know tons of people with health problems who would desire nothing more than a new body; perhaps you are one of these people. The hope that Paul and the Pauls of the world can hold onto is that one day, when Jesus returns and glorification takes place, we will have a new glorious body, a body just like Jesus possesses.

In seeing that God is not only interested in our spiritual redemption but our physical as well, the work of glorification does not stop there. Romans 8:20-21 reveals, "**²⁰For the creation was subjected to frustration, not by its own choice, but by the will of the one who subjected it, in hope ²¹that the creation itself will be set free from its bondage to corruption and obtain the freedom of the glory of the children of God.**"[198] From these verses, Paul declares that when human redemption takes place, it will lead to a redeemed creation. As we discussed previously, when Adam sinned, creation was cursed because God gave creation to Adam to oversee it. Creation's fate was connected to Adam's fate. With God through Jesus redeeming humanity, creation will be redeemed when Christ returns. There will be a day in which our eyes will behold a perfect creation because Revelation 21:1 tells us, "**¹Then I saw 'a new heaven and a new** earth' for the first heaven and the first earth had passed away, and there was no longer any sea."[199] Okay, for those of you who are lovers of the sea, you might be feeling really bummed in thinking in God's perfect world there is no sea. Let me give you some hope in that ,when John writes there is no more sea, as Alan F. Johnson in his commentary on Revelation points out, "The sea the source of the satanic beast and the place of the dead will be gone. Again, John's emphasis is not geographic but moral and spiritual. The sea serves as an archetype with connotations of evil. Thus, no trace of evil in any form will be present in the new creation."[200] As we can see here, John uses symbolic language, and he uses the sea in a symbolic way. So for all you sea lovers out there rest assured that more or likely you'll be able to enjoy the ocean when Jesus returns and sets up his kingdom. The promise and hope of glorification is found in Revelation 21:5, "**He who was seated on the throne said, 'I am making all things new!' Then he said, 'Write this down, for these words are trustworthy and true.'**"[201] God is making everything new, including you, me, and all of creation. This is the supreme joy of glorification. As John Frame so wondrously explains, "Glorification is multidimensional. It involves both individual and collective eschatology. It involves the perfecting of the spiritual nature of the individual believer, which takes place at death, when the Christian passes into the presence of the Lord. It also involves the perfecting of the bodies of all believers, which will occur at the time of the resurrection in connection with the second coming of Christ. It even involves the transformation of the entire creation."[202]

What a journey we have been on together! If you have made it to the end of this book, thank you for taking time out of your schedule to read what I have written and putting up with my jokes! In all seriousness, though, we started this journey in trying to answer two very hard questions: who is God, and who are we in relation to God? In God we see that he is the three separate people who are God the Father, God the Son, and God the Holy Spirit. And in relation to this God we are made in his image, we are fallen, and that we are in need of his glorious redemption. I hope this book might have answered some questions you have about God and about yourself. If I can give you one last encouraging thought, it is from Colossians 3:1-3, **"[1]Therefore, if you have been raised with Christ, keep seeking the things above, where Christ is, seated at the right hand of God. [2]Keep thinking about things above, not on the earth, [3]for you have died and your life is hidden with Christ in God."**[203] Keep pursuing after Jesus. The more you follow Jesus, the more the life that God desires for you will be found in him.

Bibliography

Chapter 1

Towzer, A.W. *Knowledge of the Holy.* Colorado Springs: Authentic Media, 1994

George, Timothy. "The Nature Of God: Being, Attributes, and Acts." In *A Theology Of The Church,* edited by Daniel L. Akin, 176-241. Nashville: B&H Academic, 2007

Thiessen, Henry C. *Lectures in Systematic Theology.* Revised by Vernon D. Doerksen Grand Rapids: William B. Eerdman's Publishing Company, 1979.

Driscoll, Mark, and Gerry Breshears. *Doctrine What Christians Should Believe.* Wheaton: Crossway, 2000

Lane, Tony. *A Concise History Of Christian Thought.* Grand Rapids: Baker Academic, 2006

Johnson, Alan. F. "Revelation." In *The Expositor's Bible Commentary,* edited by Kenneth L. Baker and John R. Kohlenberger III, 1125-1232. Grand Rapids: Zondervan, 1994

Erickson, Millard, J. *Introducing Christian Doctrine Second Edition.* Grand Rapids: Baker Academic, 1992

Chapter 2

Holmes, Wayne. *The Heart Of A Father.* Minneapolis: Bethany House Publishers, 2002

Grisanti, Michael. "The World Of The Old Testament." In *The World And The Word An Introduction to the Old Testament,* edited by Eugen H. Merrill, Mark F. Rooker, and Michael A. Grisanti, 13-40

Copan, Paul. *Is God a Moral Monster?* Grand Rapids: Baker Books, 2011

Kaiser, Walter. "Exodus." In *The Expositor's Bible Commentary,* edited by Kenneth L. Baker and John R. Kohlenberger III, 64-125. Grand Rapids: Zondervan, 1994

Rooker, Mark. "Jonah." *The World And The Word An Introduction to the Old Testament,* edited by Eugen H. Merrill, Mark F. Rooker, and Michael A. Grisanti, 445-452. Nashville: B&H Publishing Group, 2011

Selvaggio, Anthony. *The Prophets Speak Of Him.* Webster: Evangelical Press, 2006

Hunt, T.W. *The Doctrine Of Prayer.* Nashville: Convention Press, 1986

Lockyer, Herbert, F. F. Bruce, R. K. Harrison, Ronald Youngblood, Kermit Ecklebarger et al. *Nelson's Illustrated Bible Dictionary.* Nashville: Thomas Nelson Publishers, 1986

Keller, Timothy. *Prodigal God.* New York: Penguin Group, 2008

Abelman, Jesee. "Who Are The Macabees"? https://www.museumofthebible.org/magazine/featured/who-are-the-maccabees

Bock, Darell, L. *Luke The NIV Application Commentary.* Grand Rapids: Zondervan, 1996

Chapter 3

Saint Augustine. *Confessions.* Translated by Albert C. Outler Revised by Mark Vessey. New York: Barnes & Noble Classics, 2007

Yancey, Philip. *The Jesus I Never Knew.* Grand Rapids: Zondervan, 1995

Erickson, Millard, J. *Introducing Christian Doctrine Second Edition.* Grand Rapids: Baker Academic, 1992

Spurgeon, Charels "Morning by Morning #152: The king also crossed the Kidron Valley. 2 Samuel 15:23" From www.lifebible.com

Chaffey, Dave. "Global Social Media Statistics Research Summary May 2024" https://www.smartinsights.com/social-media-marketing/social-media-strategy/new-global-social-media-research/

Carson, D.A. "Matthew." In *The Expositor's Bible Commentary,* edited by Kenneth L. Baker and John R. Kohlenberger III, 1-135.Grand Rapids: Zondervan, 1994

Carson, D.A. *The Gospel According To John.* Grand Rapids: William B. Eerdman's Publishing Company, 1991

Oakes, John "Celsus Claimed Mary Was Impregnated By A Solider Named Pathera" https://evidenceforchristianity.org/celsus-claimed-that-mary-was-impregnated-by-a-soldier-named-pathera-comment/

www.quotefancy.com

Cicero, Tullius M. *Speech before Roman Citizens on Behalf of Gaius Rabirius, Defendant Against the Charge of Treason,* edited by William Blake Tyrell. From www.perseus.tufts.edu

Bertrand Russell, "The Free Man's Worship (1903)" https://www.users.drew.edu

Bryan Hunt "Everything Sad Will Come Untrue" https://www.stgeorgesonline.com/2016/02/17/12116/

Chapter 4

Pentecost, Dwight, J. *The Divine Comforter.* Grand Rapids: Kregel Productions, 1963

Sproul, R.C. *The Mystery Of The Holy Spirit.* Wheaton: Tyndale House Publishers, 1982

Yancey, Philip. *The Jesus I Never Knew.* Grand Rapids: Zondervan, 1995

Sanders, Fred. *The Deep Things Of God.* Wheaton: Crossway, 2010

Peterman, Gerald. "Ephesians." In *The Moody Bible Commentary,* edited by Michael Rydelnik and Michael Vanlaningham, 1845-1856. Chicago: Moody Publishers, 2014

Calvin, John. *Institutes of the Christian Religion.* Translated by Henry Beveridge. Peabody: Hendrickson Publishers, 2008

Grudem, Wayne, A. Richard B. Gaffin, Jr, Robert L. Saucy, C. Samuel Storms, and Douglass A. Oss. *Are Miraculous Gifts for Today?* Grand Rapids: Zondervan, 1996

Yancy, Philip. *Disappointment With God.* Grand Rapids: Zondervan, 1988

Zuber, Kevin, D. "1 Thessalonians." In *The Moody Bible Commentary,* edited by Michael Rydelnik and Michael Vanlaningham, 1877-1890. Chicago: Moody Publishers, 2014

Erickson, Millard, J. *Introducing Christian Doctrine Second Edition.* Grand Rapids: Baker Academic, 1992

Chapter 5

Ryrie, Charles, C. *Basic Theology.* Chicago: Moody Publishers, 1999

Roberts, Vaughn. *God's Big Picture.* Downers Grove: InterVarsity Press, 2002

Evangeline Anderson-Rajkumar, "Ministry in the Killing Fields" From www.christianhistory.org

Jennifer A. Boardman "Preaching the gospel remedy" From www.christianhistoryinstitute.org

Sailhamer, John, H. "Genesis." In *The Expositor's Bible Commentary,* edited by Kenneth L. Baker and John R. Kohlenberger III, 1-63.Grand Rapids: Zondervan, 1994

Calvin, John, *Institutes of the Christian Religion.* Ed. John T. McNeill. Trans. Ford Lewis. Battles. Philadelphia: Westminster, 1960

Beale, G. K. and Mitchell Kim. *God Dwells Among Us.* Downers Grove: InterVarsity Press, 2021

The Caged Man In The Bronx Zoo Saved By Harlem's Mount Olive Baptist Church 1906, From www.Harlemworldmagazine.com

The Inspiration Behind "My Human Pet", The Story of Ota Benga, www.Olympiablack.com

Chapter 6

https://www.newscientist.com/letter/0-the-trilemma-of-evil-in-a-classical-question/

Longman III, Tremper. *How To Read Genesis.* Downers Grove: InterVarsity Press, 2005

Burke, John, P. *Studies in Genesis.* Winona Lake: BMH Books, 1978

Jacobs, Alan. *Original Sin.* Wheaton: Harper One, 2001

Freud, Sigmund, *Civilization and Its Discontents,* trans. Joan Riviere. London: Hogarth, 1963

Erickson, Millard, J. *Introducing Christian Doctrine Second Edition.* Grand Rapids: Baker Academic, 1992

Jesse Ainslie and Joseph Lam "Manasseh" From www.Bibleodyssey.org

Jordan M. Poss, "What's Wrong, Chesterton?" From www.jordanmposs.com

Chapter 7

Lewis, C.S. *Mere Christianity.* New York: Harper One, 1952

Bainton, Roland, H. *Here I Stand.* New York: Penguin Group, 1977

Oberman, Heiko, A. *Luther: Man Between God and the Devil.* London: Yale University Press, 2006

Hopson Boutot, "Why Martin Luther Hated God" From www.poqusonbaptist.org

Keathly, Kenneth. "The Work of God: Salvation." In *A Theology Of The Church,* edited by Daniel L. Akin, 686-764. Nashville: B&H Academic, 2007

Eric Raymond, "If I Could Hear Christ Praying In The Next Room, I Would Not Fear A Million Enemies" From www.TheGospelCoalition.org

Hector Lianes, "John Newton and God's Instrument Against Oppression." From www.gcu.edu

Newton, John. *Thoughts Upon The African Slave Trade.* Middletown: Wildside Press, 2024

Bob Black, "Amazing Grace" From www.wesleyan.org

Woodall, David. "2 Corinthians." In *The Moody Bible Commentary* edited by Michael Rydelnik and Michael Vanlaningham, 1807-1825. Chicago: Moody Publishers, 2014

Johnson, Alan. "Revelation." In *The Expositor's Bible Commentary,* edited by Kenneth L. Baker and John R. Kohlenberger III, 1125-1232.Grand Rapids: Zondervan, 1994

Frame, John M. *Systematic Theology An Introduction To Christian Belief.* Philipsburg: P&R Publishers, 2013

Footnotes

1. ^ A.W. Tozer, The Knowledge Of The Holy, 1
2. ^ Timothy George, A Theology For The Church , 183
3. ^ George, 185
4. ^ Henry C. Thiessen, Lectures In Systematic Theology, 90
5. ^ Mark Driscoll and Gerry Breshears, Doctrine What Christians Should Believe, 13
6. ^ Tony A. Lane, A Concise History Of Christian Thought, 15
7. ^ Lane 17
8. ^ Driscoll and Breshers, 25
9. ^ NLT
10. ^ NIV
11. ^Alan F. Johnson, The Expositor's Bible Commentary, 1132
12. ^ Driscoll and Breshears, 29
13. ^ Millard J. Erickson, Introducing Christian Doctrine, Second Edition, 107
14. ^ Driscoll and Breshers, 12
15. ^ NIV
16. ^ Erickson107
17. ^ NIV
18. ^ Erickson, 115
19. ^ Wayne Holmes, The Heart Of A Father, 13
20. ^ Michael Grisanti, "The World Of The Old Testament" in The World And The Word: An Introduction To The Old Testament, 13
21. ^ Paul Copan, Is God a Moral Monster? 21
22. ^ NET
23. ^ Walter C Kaiser Jr, "Exodus" In The Expositor's Bible Commentary, 122
24. ^ NIV
25. ^ Mark F Rooker, "Jonah", From The World And The Word An Introduction to the Old Testament, 450
26. ^ Anthony Selvaggio, The Prophets Speak Of Him, 71
27. ^ T. W. Hunt, The Doctrine Of Prayer, 8
28. ^ NIV

29. ^ NIV

30. ^ NIV

31. ^ Selvaggio, 73

32. ^ NIV

33. ^ NIV

34. ^ NIV

35. ^ NIV

36. ^ Rooker, 417

37. ^ NIV

38. ^ NLT

39. ^ Selvaggio, 18

40. ^ NLT

41. ^ NLT

42. ^ NIV

43. ^ NIV

44. ^ NIV

45. ^ Herbert Lockyer, Sr, Nelson's Illustrated Bible Dictionary, 1032

46. ^ Timothy Keller, Prodigal God, 8

47. ^ Lockyer, 830

48. ^ Jesse Abelman, Who Are The Maccabees, Museumofthebible.org

49. ^ NIV

50. ^ NIV

51. ^ Darrell L Bock, "Luke", in the NIV Application Commentary, 413

52. ^ NIV

53. ^ Luke 15:31-32, NIV

54. ^ NIV John 21:25

55. ^ NIV

56. ^ NET

57. ^ Saint Augustine of Hippo, Confessions 1, 1.5

58. ^ Philip Yancey, The Jesus I Never Knew, 36

59. ^ NET John 1:10

60. ^ NLT John 1:33-34

61. ^ NLT Isaiah 53:2

62. ^ NET John 1:11

63. ^ Yancey, 34

64. ^ NET Matthew 2:18

65. ^ Erickson, 234

66. ^ NIV Matthew 4:1

67. ^ NIV Matthew 6:13

68. ^ NLT Philippians 2:6-7

69. ^ NLT Matthew 24:36

70. ^ Charels Spurgeon, "Morning by Morning #152: The king also crossed the Kidron Valley. 2 Samuel 15:23" From www.lifebible.com

71. ^ NIV

72. ^ ESV Translation

73. ^ Globa Social Media Statistics Research Summary 2024, www.smartinsights.com

74. ^ NET Matthew 26:38

75. ^ D.A. Carson, "Matthew", The Expositor's Bible Commentary, 82

76. ^ Mark 3:17

77. ^ NET Luke 9:54

78. ^ KJV Luke 9:56

79. ^ NLT

80. ^ NLT

81. ^ ESV John 8:41

82. ^ D.A. Carson, The Gospel According To John, 352

83. ^ Dr. John Oakes, "Celsus Claimed Mary Was Impregnated By A Solider Named Pathera" www.evidenceforchristianity.org

84. ^ NLT

85. ^ NLT

86. ^ NET Matthew 10:34-36

87. ^ NLT Matthew 11:11

88. ^ Quotefancy.com

89. ^ M. Tullius Cicero, Speech before Roman Citizens on Behalf of Gaius Rabirius, Defendant Against the Charge of Treason, edited by William Blake Tyrell. From perseus.tufts.edu

90. ^ NLT Hebrews 12:2

91. ^ NIV 1st Corinthians 15:17

92. ^ Bertrand Russell, "The Free Man's Worship (1903)" https://www.users.drew.edu

93. ^ Bryan Hunt "Everything Sad Will Come Untrue" https://www.stgeorgesonline.com/2016/02/17/12116/

94. ^ J. Dwight Pentecost, The Divine Comforter: The Person and Work of the Holy Spirit, 11

95. ^ Yancey, 228

96. ^ NIV

97. ^ESV John 16:5-7

98. ^ RC Sproul, The Mystery Of The Holy Spirit, 182

99. ^ NLT

100. ^ Fred Sanders, The Deep Things Of God, 30

101. ^ Sanders, pg31

102. ^ NIV

103. ^ NIV

104.   ^ NIV Psalm 51:11

105.   ^ NIV

106.   ^ Gerald Peterman, "Ephesians", The Moody Bible Commentary, 1848

107.   ^ John Calvin, The Institutes Of The Christian Religion, 349

108.   ^ NET

109.   ^ Robert L Saucy, Are Miraculous Gifts For Today, 103

110.   ^ Philip Yancey, Disappointment With God, 89-90

111.   ^ Saucy, 114

112.   ^ Saucy, 105

113.   ^ Kevin D. Zuber, "1 Thessalonians", The Moody Bible Commentary, 1889

114.   ^ NLT

115.   ^ NIV

116.   ^ NIV

117.   ^ ESV Philippians 2:13

118.   ^ Erickson, 270

119.   ^ Charels C. Ryrie, Basic Theology, 216

120.   ^ NIV

121.   ^ Vaugh Roberts, God's Big Picture, 28

122.   ^ NET James 2:14-18

123.   ^ Evangeline Anderson-Rajkumar, "Ministry in the Killing Fields" From www.christianhistory.org

124.   ^ Jennifer A. Boardman "Preaching the gospel remedy" From www.christianhistoryinstitute.org

125.   ^ NIV Psalm 8:3-5

126.   ^ NIV Hebrews 1:4

127.   ^ NIV

128.   ^ NIV 1st Peter 1:12

129.   ^ NIV

130.   ^ NIV

131.   ^ John H. Sailhamer, Genesis, The Expositor's Bible Commentary, pg 7

132.   ^ John Calvin, Institutes of the Christian Religion. Ed. John T. McNeill. Trans. Ford Lewis. Battles. Philadelphia, PA: Westminster, 1960. p. 108. Print. [Institutes 1.11.8; References were reformatted and paragraph breaks were added for readability]

133.   ^ NIV Ecclesiastes 1:2

134.   ^ NIV Matthew 28:18-20

135.   ^ G.K. Beale and Mitchell Kim, God Dwells Among Us, 18

136.   ^ Beale and Kim, 18

137.   ^ NIV

138.   ^ NIV

139.   ^ The Caged Man In The Bronx Zoo Saved By Harlem's Mount Olive Baptist Church 1906, website www.Harlemworldmagazine.com

140. ^ The Inspiration Behind "My Human Pet", The Story of Ota Benga, www.Olympiablack.com

141. ^ NIV

142. ^ https://www.newscientist.com/letter/0-the-trilemma-of-evil-in-a-classical-question/

143. ^ NLT Habakkuk 1:2-3

144. ^ Tremper Long, How To Read Genesis, 72

145. ^ John P Burke, Studies In Genesis, 35

146. ^ NIV Genesis 3:1-3

147. ^ NLT

148. ^ NIV Genesis 3:15

149. ^ NIV Genesis 3:16

150. ^ ESV

151. ^NIV Genesis 3:17-19

152. ^ NIV

153. ^ NIV

154. ^ NET

155. ^ Alan Jacobs, Original Sin, Introduction

156. ^ Sigmund Freud, Civilization and Its Discontents, 58.

157. ^ NIV Genesis 8:21

158. ^ NIV

159. ^ Erickson, 188-89

160. ^ NIV

161. ^ NIV

162. ^ NLT

163. ^ Jesse Ainslie and Joseph Lam "Manasseh" www.Bibleodyssey.org

164. ^ Jordan M. Poss, What's Wrong, Chesterton? www.jordanmposs.com

165. ^ NLT

166. ^ NIV

167. ^ NIV

168. ^ ESV

169. ^ ESV

170. ^C. S. Lewis, Mere Christianity, 31

171. ^ Lewis, 63

172. ^ NIV

173. ^ NLT

174. ^ Roland H. Bainton, Here I Stand, 15

175. ^ Luther: Man Between God and the Devil, 315

176. ^ Hopson Boutot, "Why Martin Luther Hated God" From www.poquson-baptist.org

177. ^ ESV

178. ^ Bainton, 49-50

179.   ^ Keathly, 701

180.   ^ NLT

181.   ^ ESV

182.   ^ NLT

183.   ^ Eric Raymond, "If I Could Hear Christ Praying In The Next Room, I Would Not Fear A Million Enemies" www.TheGospelCoalition.org

184.   ^ Hector Lianes, "John Newton and God's Instrument Against Oppression." From www.gcu.edu

185.   ^ Lianes

186.   ^ John Newton, Thoughts Upon The African Slave Trade, 05

187.   ^ Bob Black, "Amazing Grace" From www.wesleayn.org

188.   ^ ESV

189.   ^ NIV

190.   ^ ESV

191.   ^ NIV Matthew 22:37-38

192.   ^ ESV

193.   ^ NLT

194.   ^ NIV Romans 8:11

195.   ^ NIV Philippians 3:20-21

196.   ^ NIV

197.   ^ David Woodall, 2 Corinthians in The Moody Bible Commentary, 1823

198.   ^ ESV

199.   ^ NIV

200.   ^ Johnson, 1225

201.   ^ NIV

202.   ^ John M. Frame, Systematic Theology: An Introduction To Christian Belief, 334

203.   ^ NET

Daryl C. Cyrus Jr. (M.A. in Biblical Studies and Theology from Belhaven University, Summer 2024) is a follower of Jesus Christ who has worked in various ministry settings. With twenty years of ministry experience both as a staff member and as a volunteer, Daryl is passionate about helping people better know God and themselves.